Oracle Stored Programs for Beginners

Creating Your Own Procedures and Functions in PL/SQL

Djoni Darmawikarta

Table of Contents

Introduction

Welcome to *Oracle Stored Programs for Beginners: Creating Your Own Procedures and Functions in PL/SQL*. This book is for you if you want to learn Oracle stored programs the easy way. By particularly following the book examples you will quickly gain practical skills.

You write a stored program in PL/SQL. When you successfully compile the PL/SQL source code, the resulting program, which is a database object, is stored in the database (hence the name *stored* program). Other programs and other users that have the permission can then use the stored program.

A stored program can be a procedure or function. It can have both SQL and procedural statements. The SQL statements are used to access *sets* of data stored in the database, while the procedural statements are used to process *individual* data item, and to control the program flow using the if-then-else and looping structures.

About This Book

This book consists of eight chapters and three appendixes. This section gives you an overview of each chapter and appendixes.

Chapter 1, "Stored Procedure Basics", walks you through the fundamental structure and features of stored procedure.

Chapter 2, "Controlling Program Flow", covers the procedural constructs, including if, if-then, loop, and case.

Chapter 3, "Using SQL in Stored Procedure", shows you especially how to imbed SQL statements in your procedures.

Chapter 4, "Cursor", teaches you how a procedure can handle multiple rows return from an SQL query.

Chapter 5, "Exception Handling", discusses a feature used to handle run-time error.

Chapter 6, "Creating Stored Function", introduces stored function; you will learn how to create and use stored function in this chapter.

Chapter 7, "Package", is about packaging related procedures and/or functions.

Chapter 8, "Permission", shows how you should properly authorize others who need to use your stored programs.

Appendix A, "Installing Oracle Database Express Edition", is your step-by-step guide to install MySQL Community Edition.

Appendix B, "Introduces inline programs" gives you an idea about the procedure and function that you can write inside a PL/SQL program.

Appendix C, "Source Codes", has all the source codes of the book examples for your use.

Chapter 1: Stored Procedure Basics

Stored procedure is a database object. You create a stored procedure using the CREATE PROCEDURE statement. The SQL statement has the following syntax.

```
CREATE PROCEDURE procedure_name(parameters) AS
BEGIN
declaration_statements;
.  .  .
executable_statements;
.  .  .
END procedure_name;
```

The procedure specification has declaration and executable statements located within the BEGIN … END block.

Parameters and declaration statement are optional.

A stored procedure must have at least one executable statement.

Every declaration statement and executable statement must be terminated by a semicolon (;)

Creating Stored Procedure in SQL Developer

To create a new procedure, right-click the Procedures folder under your connection; and then select the New Procedure.

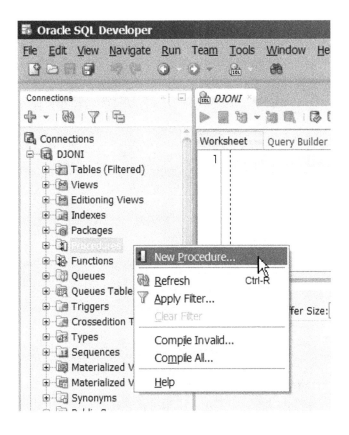

A Create Procedure window will appear.

Change the name of the procedure to the name of your procedure; for example, *do_nothing*, then click the OK button.

You will get a skeleton of the procedure be on the worksheet. It has only a NULL statement, a statement that does nothing.

You will notice the CREATE is followed by an optional OR REPLACE. If you have the OR REPLACE option and you already have a stored procedure with the same name, the existing will be updated when you run the statement.

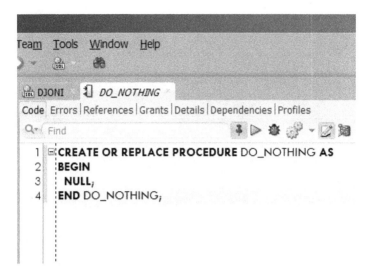

To compile the source code, click the Compile menu item.

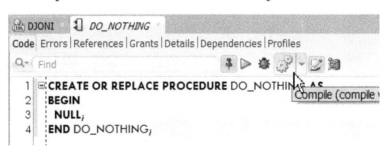

Your compilation is successful if you see the "Compiled" message on the Message - Log pane (bottom right-hand corner pane). In the Connections pane, the hello_world procedure is listed under the Procedures folder; it is now a stored procedure, an object within the database (the database defined in the connection).

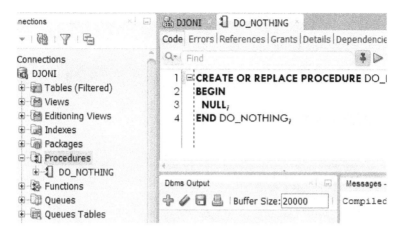

To test the procedure, run an EXECUTE statement on it. Note that the parentheses are optional, as the procedure does not have any parameter.

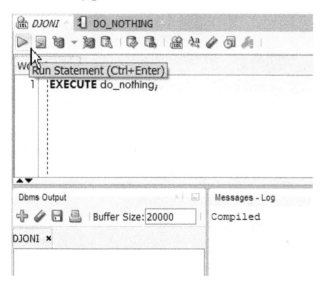

You will see a message a successful completion message on the Script Output pane.

You can use a stored procedure the same way you use any built-in procedure. In a PL/SQL program for example, you just write the name of the procedure with its parameter if it has any.

Hello World

Without further ado, let's create our first stored procedure that *does* something, showing nothing else than the customary "Hello, World" greeting as an introduction to a programming language.

Follow the same steps when you created the do_nothing stored procedure. Name our procedure hello_world. Replace the NULL statement with dbms_output.put_line('Hello, World').

In this book we use the built-in dbms_output.put_line as we want to see immediate output, to check if our procedure works as expected. In real-world procedures you can use dbms_output.put_line statements during development for testing and debugging.

When you use the hello_world procedure after successfully compiling it, you should see the expected output, the "Hello, World" displayed on the Dbms Output pane.

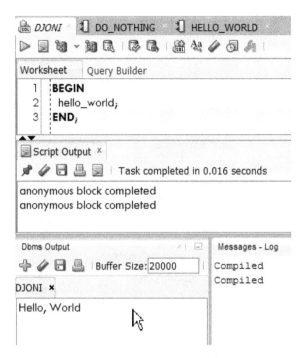

To modify a procedure, right click the procedure. Edit the procedure as you need, the compile it.

To delete a procedure from the database, right click the procedure then click Drop.

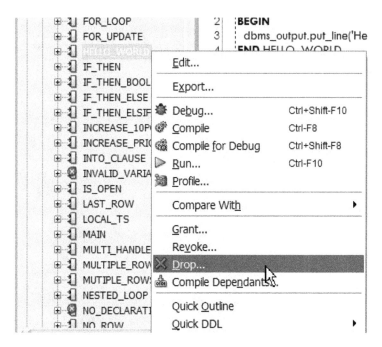

You will be requested to confirm the deletion. If you are sure click the Apply button. On the next confirmation window, click OK to close it. The procedure will no longer be available.

Name of Procedure

You must observe the following rules when naming a procedure.

- Can contain only letters (a-z, A-Z), digits 0-9, dollar sign ($), pound sign (#) and underscore (_)
- Starts with an alpha character
- Has a maximum length of 30 characters
- Must be unique within the database

When you try an invalid name, for example, a name that starts with a numeric or already exists, you will be warned.

Updating Procedure

You can update an existing procedure by right-clicking the procedure.

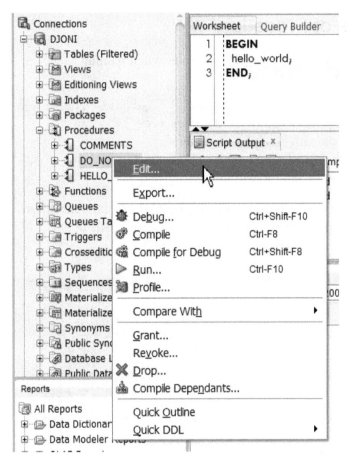

When you finish editing the procedure, you need to compile it; the existing stored procedure will be replaced.

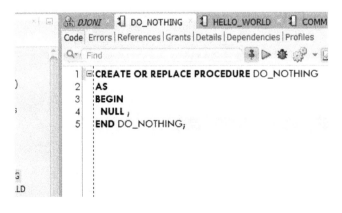

Deleting Procedure

To delete a procedure, right click the procedure; then select Drop.

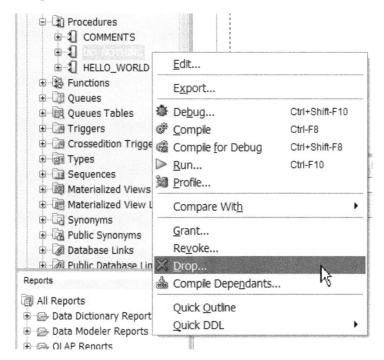

Confirm by clicking the Apply button.

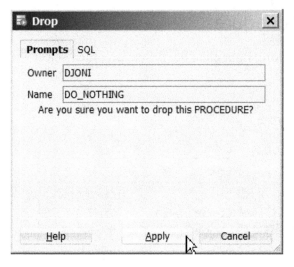

Close the Confirmation window by clicking its OK button.

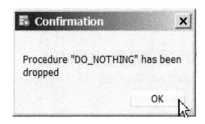

The procedure will no longer be in the Procedure folder.

Comment

A short break here before we explore further functional features of stored program.

Comment lines within the source code can be useful as inline documentation. Comments are ignored by the compiler.

Comment comes in two flavours: Single and multi-line. Any text in a source code following a double dash -- until the end of the line, is a single-line comment.

When a / * mark is encountered, all texts and lines until a closing * / mark is a multi-line comment.

```
1  CREATE OR REPLACE PROCEDURE COMMENTS
2  AS
3     /* An example stored procedure to show the two types of comment lines.
4     This one is a multi-line comment
5     */
6  BEGIN
7     -- Use the built-in procedure to display a string ( single-line comment)
8     dbms_output.put_line( 'Hello, World'); -- a Hello, World (another single-line comment)
9  END COMMENTS;
```

Declaring Variable

The statement syntax to declare a variable is:

```
DECLARE variable_name datatype DEFAULT value;
```

The datatype is mandatory; DEFAULT is optional.
  A variable name can contain only letters (a-z, A-Z), digits 0-9, dollar sign ($), pound sign (#) and underscore (_) and must start with an alpha character

When you try an invalid name, the source code will fail to compile. The Compiler – Log shows an error message.

Displaying Variable

The parameter of a SELECT statement does not need to be a *literal*. In the following display_variable procedure the parameter is the greeting variable. The string literal stored in the greeting variable, Hello World!, will be displayed. The Hello World! Value gets stored in the greeting variable during its declaration thanks to the **DEFAULT** clause.

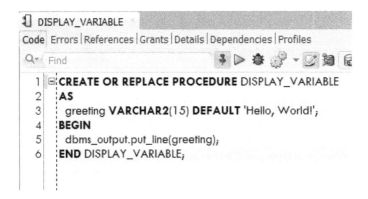

Data Type

When you declare a variable you must specify its type. You have seen the use of VARCHAR2 data type, used to store variable length string of characters.

Other commonly used data types are:

- CHAR (m) - to store a fixed length string of characters to a maximum of m characters.
- INTEGER - to store numeric integer type of data
- DECIMAL (p, s) - to store numeric data with precision of p digits and scale of s digits
- DATE – to store date
- TIMESTAMP– to store date and time

The following data_types procedure shows the use of the above first four data types.

```
DATA_TYPES

Code  Errors | References | Grants | Details | Dependencies | Profiles

Find

 1   CREATE OR REPLACE PROCEDURE DATA_TYPES
 2   AS
 3     c VARCHAR(5) DEFAULT 'MySQL';
 4     i INTEGER(2) DEFAULT 99;
 5     n NUMBER(4,2) DEFAULT 23.45;
 6     dt DATE DEFAULT '2014-09-20';
 7   BEGIN
 8     dbms_output.put_line(c);
 9     dbms_output.put_line(i);
10     dbms_output.put_line(n);
11     dbms_output.put_line(dt);
12   END DATA_TYPES;
```

Here is an example of the use of TIMESTAMP variable. localtimestamp is a built-in function that returns your computer date and time at the time you call the procedure.

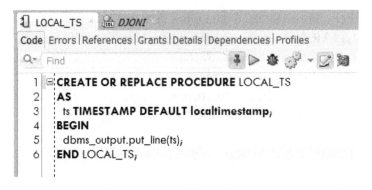

Variable must be declared

You must declare a variable before you can use it in an executable statement.

In the following no_declaration procedure, the *greeting* variable is not declared. When you compile the procedure, you will get an error message.

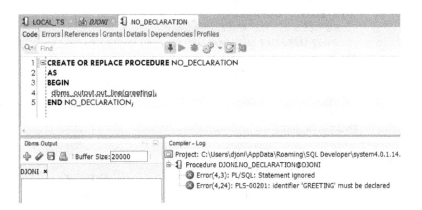

Setting Variable Value

You assign a value to a variable value using := operator.

```
SET variable := value;
```

The *value* can be a literal (data value), variable or expression.

In the following set_var procedure the value 'PL/SQL' of variable w is changed to 'Welcome to PL/SQL'. In this statement the *value* is an expression CONCAT('Welcome to ', w).

You also use the := assignment operator for storing the result of numeric computation. In the following computation procedure, the * is a multiplication operator; power is a function that raises the ((x - 0.1) * 5 + (z + 0.9) to the power of 2, i.e. 7 to the power of 2; hence, y is 49.

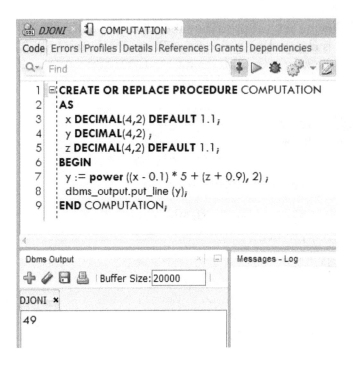

Interacting with Database

To interact with the database, you use SQL statements in the procedure.

Note that this book does not specifically cover SQL. To quickly gain SQL skill, read my book, *"Oracle SQL"*

The following sql_statements procedure has an INSERT, UPDATE and DELETE SQL statements. The statements change the rows of the product table.

```
1  CREATE OR REPLACE PROCEDURE SQL_STATEMENTS
2  AS
3  BEGIN
4   INSERT INTO product VALUES
5    (9999, 'Test', NULL, NULL, NULL
6    );
7   UPDATE product SET price = 0 WHERE p_code = 9999;
8   DELETE FROM product WHERE p_code = 9;
9  END SQL_STATEMENTS;
```

To try the example, you need to create the product table by executing the following SQL statement.

```
CREATE TABLE product
(p_code INTEGER PRIMARY KEY,
p_name VARCHAR2(20),
p_type CHAR(6),
price NUMBER(4,2),
update_dt DATE);
```

To run the statement click the Run Statement button.

```
1  CREATE TABLE produce
2  (code INTEGER PRIMARY KEY,
3  name VARCHAR2(20),
4  type CHAR(6),
5  price NUMBER(4,2),
6  update_dt DATE);
7
```

Then, insert the six rows into the table by executing the following six SQL statements.

```
INSERT INTO product VALUES(1,
    'Apple','Fruit',1,to_date('1-MAY-2014','DD-MON-
    YYYY'));
```

```
INSERT INTO product
        VALUES(2,'Broccoli','Veggie',2,to_date('2-MAY-
        2014','DD-MON-YYYY'));
INSERT INTO product VALUES(3
        ,'Carrot','Veggie',3,to_date('3-MAY-2014','DD-
        MON-YYYY'));
INSERT INTO product
        VALUES(4,'Mango','Fruit',4,to_date('4-MAY-
        2014','DD-MON-YYYY'));
INSERT INTO product
        VALUES(5,'Grape','Fruit',5,to_date('5-MAY-
        2014','DD-MON-YYYY'));
INSERT INTO product VALUES(9,NULL,NULL,NULL,NULL);
```

To execute all the statements at once, click the Run Script button.

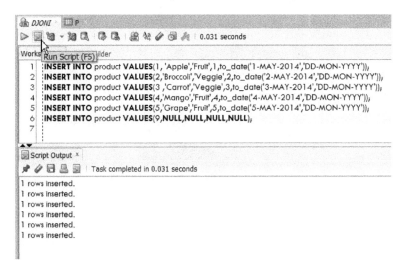

Here are the rows before you call the procedure.

	P_CODE	P_NAME	P_TYPE	PRICE	LAUNCH_DT
1	1 Apple	Fruit	1	14-05-01
2	2 Broccoli	Veggie	2	14-05-02
3	3 Carrot	Veggie	3	14-05-03
4	4 Mango	Fruit	4	14-05-04
5	5 Grape	Fruit	5	14-05-05
6	9 (null)	(null)	(null)	(null)

After calling the procedure, the rows will be as follows.

	P_CODE	P_NAME	P_TYPE	PRICE	LAUNCH_DT
1	1 Apple	Fruit	1	14-05-01
2	2 Broccoli	Veggie	2	14-05-02
3	3 Carrot	Veggie	3	14-05-03
4	4 Mango	Fruit	4	14-05-04
5	5 Grape	Fruit	5	14-05-05
6	9999 Test	(null)	0	(null)

Parameter

Recall the syntax of the CREATE PROCEDURE statement:

```
CREATE PROCEDURE procedure_name(parameters) AS
BEGIN
declaration_statements;
. . .
executable_statements;
. . .
END procedure_name;
```

You can pass data when you call a procedure that has parameters defined for the data. The following increase_price procedure has two parameters; the first is the code of the product you want to increase the price and the increase in percentage.

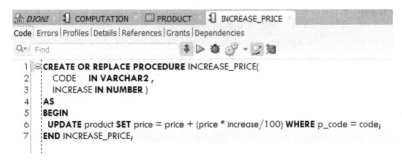

On the Create Procedure window, you specify a parameter by clicking the green + sign.

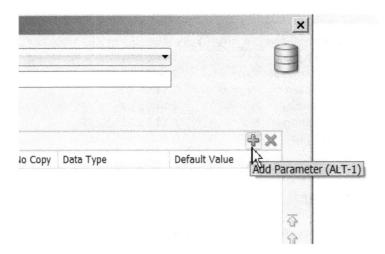

Change the name of the PARAM1 suggested; click the + sign again to add a second parameter. Note that you must define the datatype of the parameter.

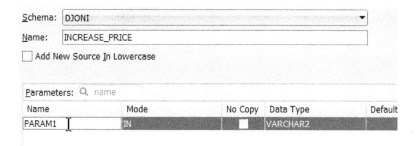

When you have entered the two parameters of the increase_price procedure, your window should look like the following. Then, click the OK button.

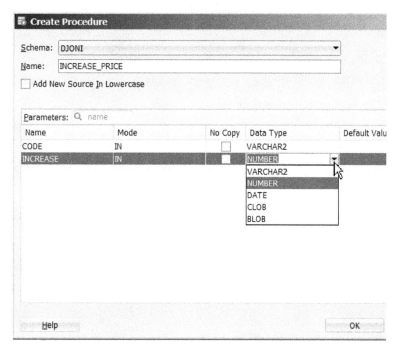

You should now have the increase_price skeletion on the worksheet.

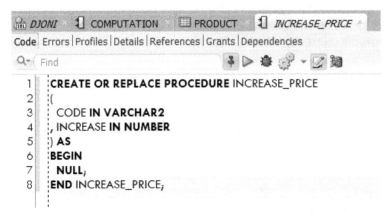

Replace the NULL; executable statement with the UPDATE statement. Then compile the procedure.

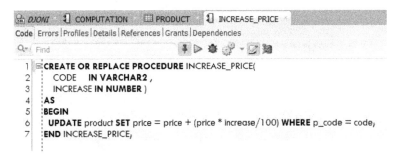

When you call the procedure you must supply the values for the parameters.

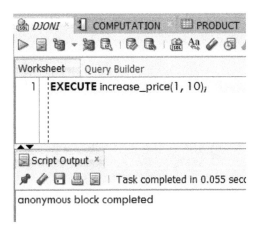

Assuming the rows of the product table are as follows

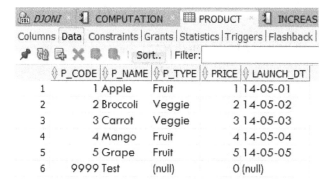

After the call to the increase_procedure, the Apple's price will increase to 1.10

Calling within Procedure

You can call a procedure within another procedure. The following main procedure has three of the procedures we already created earlier.

```
1  ⊟ CREATE OR REPLACE PROCEDURE MAIN
2    AS
3    BEGIN
4      hello_world;
5      data_types;
6      display_variable;
7    END MAIN;
```

Dbms Output

Buffer Size: 20000

Messages - Log

Compiled

DJONI ×

```
Hello, World
MySQL
99
23.45
14-09-20
Hello, World!
```

Chapter 2: Controlling Program Flow

The executable statements in all preceding examples are executed linearly from top to the bottom of the programs. In this chapter you will learn conditional and loop statements to control the execution flow of a program.

Control Statements

To control program flows, you use conditional and loop statements.

IF THEN

The syntax of the IF THEN statement is.

```
IF condition THEN
   statements;
END IF;
```

Only if the condition is true the statements will be executed.

The following IF_THEN procedure will display the value of num_input parameter only if it is > 10.

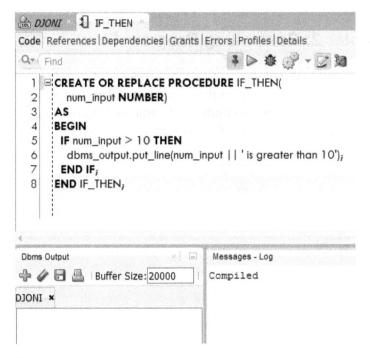

When you execute the procedure passing 10.1, it will be displayed.

Boolean datatype

A Boolean variable can be true or false.

While in the previous if_then procedure, the IF condition is hardcoded, the following procedure uses a Boolean variable, greater_than_10, as the condition. The variable is declared as true when num_input is greater than 10. This true condition is then you as the condition on the if statement.

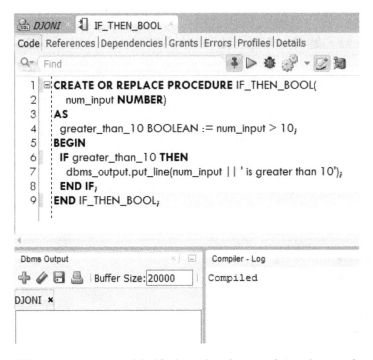

When you execute this if_then_bool procedure, the result will be the same as that of the if_then procedure.

IF THEN ELSE

The syntax of the IF THEN ELSE statement is.

```
IF condition THEN
   if_statements;
ELSE
   else_statements;
END IF;
```

An IF THEN ELSE executes its if_statements if its condition is true. If the condition is false, the else_statements are executed.

The following IF THEN ELSE procedure displays either greater than or less than 10, depending on the parameter value you pass when you execute the procedure.

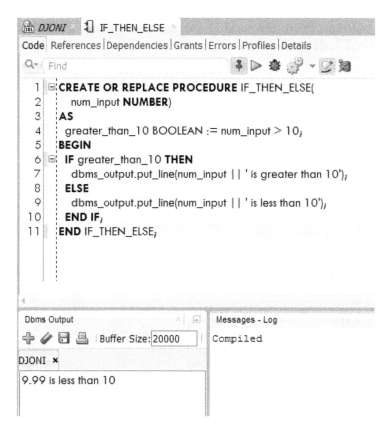

IF THEN ELSIF

If you need multiple ELSE's, then use an IF THEN ELSIF statement. Its syntax is as follows.

```
IF condition_1 THEN
   statements_1;
ELSIF condition_2 THEN
   statements_2;
ELSIF ...
[ ELSE
   else_statements ]
END IF;
```

The IF THEN ELSIF statement executes only the first statement for which its condition is true; the remaining conditions are not evaluated. If no condition is true, then the else_statements are executed, if they exist; otherwise, the IF THEN ELSIF statement does nothing.

The ELSE is optional.

The following IF_THEN_ELSIF procedure demonstrates the use of the IF THEN ELSIF statement.

```
DJONI    IF_THEN_ELSIF
Code  References | Dependencies | Grants | Errors | Profiles | Details
Q  Find

 1  CREATE OR REPLACE PROCEDURE IF_THEN_ELSIF(
 2      num_input NUMBER)
 3  AS
 4      greater_than_10 BOOLEAN := num_input > 10;
 5  BEGIN
 6      IF greater_than_10 THEN
 7          dbms_output.put_line(num_input || ' is greater than 10');
 8      ELSIF num_input = 10 THEN
 9          dbms_output.put_line(num_input || ' is equal to 10');
10      ELSE
11          dbms_output.put_line(num_input || ' is less than 10');
12      END IF;
13  END IF_THEN_ELSIF;
```

```
Dbms Output                          ×  ⊟      Messages - Log
          Buffer Size: 20000
DJONI ×
10 is equal to 10
```

Simple CASE

The syntax of the Simple CASE statement is.
```
CASE selector
WHEN selector_value_1 THEN statements_1
WHEN selector_value_2 THEN statements_2
WHEN ...
[ ELSE else_statements ]
END CASE;
```

The selector is a variable. Each selector_value can be either a literal or a variable.

The simple CASE statement runs the first statement for which its selector_value equals the selector. Remaining conditions are not evaluated. If no selector_value equals selector, the CASE statement runs else_statements if they exist; or raises the predefined exception CASE_NOT_FOUND otherwise.

The ELSE is optional.

The selector in the following SIMPLE_CASE procedure is a variable named *clue*. The statement has four WHEN's, each with a literal as its selector value; the first WHEN's selector value, for example, is literal 'O'. If the clue value you enter on the prompt is not any one of the selector value's, the ELSE statement will be executed.

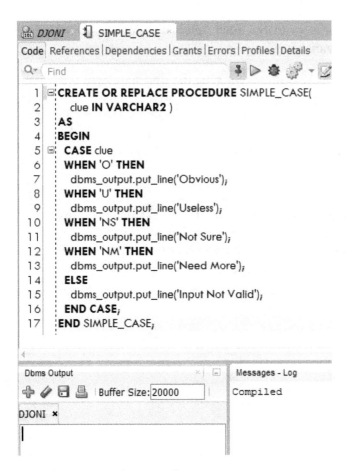

Here is an example execution.

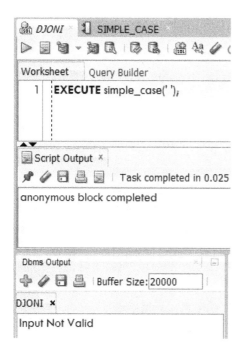

Searched CASE

A Searched CASE statement has the following syntax.

```
CASE
WHEN condition_1 THEN statements_1
WHEN condition_2 THEN statements_2
WHEN...
ELSE else_statements
END CASE;
```

The searched CASE statement executes the first statement for which its condition is true. Remaining conditions are not evaluated. If no condition is true, the CASE statement runs else_statements if they exist and raises the predefined exception CASE_NOT_FOUND otherwise.

While in the Simple CASE, the "condition" of selecting which statements to execute is comparing the selection_value to the selector for equality, in Searched CASE the condition is within each WHEN.

The conditions are independent; they do not need to have any kind of relationship.

Two or more conditions can be true, but only the first in the order you have in the source program (top to bottom) will be granted and its statements executed.

Assuming our product table has the following rows.

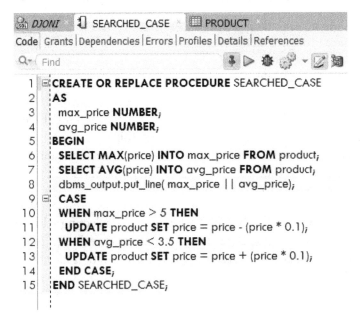

In the following searched_case procedure, the first condition is false and the second condition is true. As a result the prices get updated as shown here.

```
1  CREATE OR REPLACE PROCEDURE SEARCHED_CASE
2  AS
3    max_price NUMBER;
4    avg_price NUMBER;
5  BEGIN
6    SELECT MAX(price) INTO max_price FROM product;
7    SELECT AVG(price) INTO avg_price FROM product;
8    dbms_output.put_line( max_price || avg_price);
9    CASE
10   WHEN max_price > 5 THEN
11     UPDATE product SET price = price - (price * 0.1);
12   WHEN avg_price < 3.5 THEN
13     UPDATE product SET price = price + (price * 0.1);
14   END CASE;
15 END SEARCHED_CASE;
```

The prices after executing the searched_case procedure are as follows.

	P_CODE	P_NAME	P_TYPE	PRICE	LAUNCH_DT
1	1	Apple	Fruit	1.1	14-05-01
2	2	Broccoli	Veggie	2.2	14-05-02
3	3	Carrot	Veggie	3.3	14-05-03
4	4	Mango	Fruit	4.4	14-05-04
5	5	Grape	Fruit	5.5	14-05-05

Tab bar: DJONI | SEARCHED_CASE | PRODUCT
Columns | Data | Constraints | Grants | Statistics | Triggers | Flashback | Depen
Sort.. | Filter:

Basic LOOP

The structure of the Basic LOOP is

```
<<label>> LOOP
statements
END LOOP;
```

The statements run from the first to the last before the END LOOP, and then back to the first, until an EXIT conditional statement, which should be provided within the loop, is satisfied on which the loop is terminated.

The label is optional, but it helps clarifies the scope of the loop.

The loop in the following basic_loop procedure iterates statements on line 9 – 10 three times. On the fourth iteration num = 4, hence the exit condition is satisfied, the next statement after the loop on line 13 is executed, and then the program ends.

Nested LOOP

You can nest a loop. In the following nested_loop procedure, the inner loop on line 13 - 17 is nested within the outer loop that starts on line 5. For every iteration of the outer loop, the inner loop is iterated twice.

```
1  ⊟CREATE OR REPLACE PROCEDURE NESTED_LOOP
2   AS
3     counter1 NUMBER := 1;
4     counter2 NUMBER := 1;
5   BEGIN
6  ⊟  LOOP
7       IF counter1 > 2 THEN
8         EXIT; -- loop twice
9       END IF;
10      DBMS_OUTPUT.PUT_LINE ('Outer loop: counter1 = ' || TO_CHAR(counter1));
11      counter1 := counter1 + 1;
12 ⊟    LOOP
13        IF counter2 > 2 THEN
14          EXIT; -- loop twice
15        END IF;
16        DBMS_OUTPUT.PUT_LINE ('Inner loop: counter2 = ' || TO_CHAR(counter2));
17        counter2 := counter2 + 1;
18      END LOOP;
19      counter2 := 1;
20    END LOOP;
21    DBMS_OUTPUT.PUT_LINE('After loop: counter1 = ' || TO_CHAR(counter1));
22  END NESTED_LOOP;
```

Dbms Output | Messages - Log

Buffer Size: 20000 | Compiled

DJONI ✕

```
Outer loop: counter1 = 1
Inner loop: counter2 = 1
Inner loop: counter2 = 2
Outer loop: counter1 = 2
Inner loop: counter2 = 1
Inner loop: counter2 = 2
After loop: counter1 = 3
```

Fixed Iteration

If you know exactly the number of iteration you want, you can use the following loop structure.

```
FOR i IN l..u
  LOOP
    statements;
  END LOOP;
```

i the loop index, l the lower bound and u is the upper bound of the index. The index value starts with l when the loop is entered, and increments by 1; the last iteration is when the index reaches u.

In the following fixed_iteration procedure, as i= 1 and u = 3 the dbms_output.put_line statement inside the loop is executed three times.

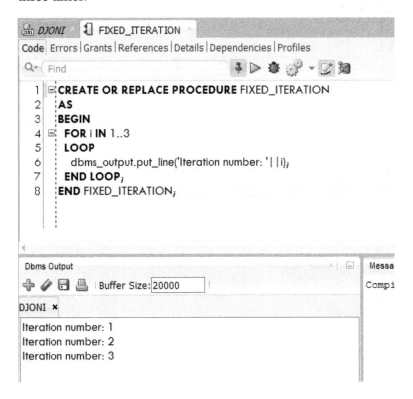

WHILE loop

You can also use a WHILE to form a loop. Its syntax is as follows.

```
WHILE condition LOOP
statements;
END LOOP;
```

The statements in the loop will be executed as long as the condition is true. You must ensure the loop can terminate.

The following while_loop procedure functions the same as the previous fixed_iteration procedure; its loop terminates when i = 4. Notice that the i variable used in this while_loop procedure must be declared; while with LOOP as in the fixed_iteration should not be. The i variable is incremented on line 8, which will terminate the loop when its value reaches 4.

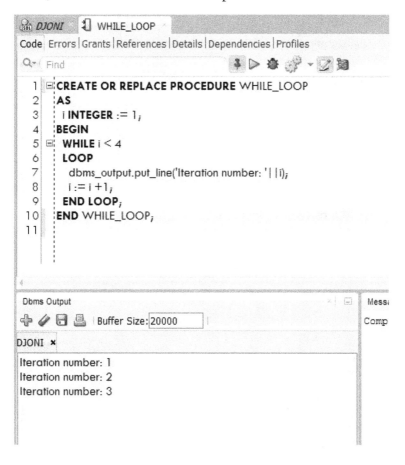

Chapter 3: Using SQL in Stored Procedure

You have seen in the previous examples that PL/SQL programs can have both *procedural statements* and *SQL statements*. In this chapter we will focus on the SQL statements used in PL/SQL programs.

The following *increase_10pct* procedure increases the prices by 10% of the average price, but only on those prices lower than average unit price.

The program has two SQL statements, a SELECT statement and an UPDATE statement.

```
DJONI    INCREASE_10PCT    PRODUCT
Code  Errors | References | Dependencies | Grants | Profiles | Details
Find

1  CREATE OR REPLACE PROCEDURE INCREASE_10PCT
2  AS
3     avg_price NUMBER;
4  BEGIN
5     SELECT AVG(price) INTO avg_price FROM product;
6     dbms_output.put_line('The average price is: ' || avg_price);
7     UPDATE product SET price = price + 0.10 * avg_price WHERE price < avg_price;
8  END INCREASE_10PCT;
9
```

Assuming our product table has the following rows.

```
DJONI    INCREASE_10PCT    PRODUCT
Columns | Data | Constraints | Grants | Statistics | Triggers | Flashback | Depe
                           Sort..   Filter:
```

	P_CODE	P_NAME	P_TYPE	PRICE	LAUNCH_DT
1	1	Apple	Fruit	1	14-05-01
2	2	Broccoli	Veggie	2	14-05-02
3	3	Carrot	Veggie	3	14-05-03
4	4	Mango	Fruit	4	14-05-04
5	5	Grape	Fruit	5	14-05-05

When you execute the increase_10pct procedure, the prices of the Apple and Broccoli increase by 10% of the average of all product prices.

	P_CODE	P_NAME	P_TYPE	PRICE	LAUNCH_DT
1	1	Apple	Fruit	1.3	14-05-01
2	2	Broccoli	Veggie	2.3	14-05-02
3	3	Carrot	Veggie	3	14-05-03
4	4	Mango	Fruit	4	14-05-04
5	5	Grape	Fruit	5	14-05-05

Dbms Output — Buffer Size: 20000

Messages - Log — Compiled

DJONI ✕

The average price is: 3

INTO clause

Note that the SELECT statement must have an INTO clause, which is not applicable in a standalone SQL query.

The SELECT with INTO syntax is

```
SELECT select_columns INTO into_columns FROM ...
```

The into_columns must be in the sequence and the same datatype as those of the select_columns.

The following *into_clause* procedure has a SELECT statement that has three INTO columns.

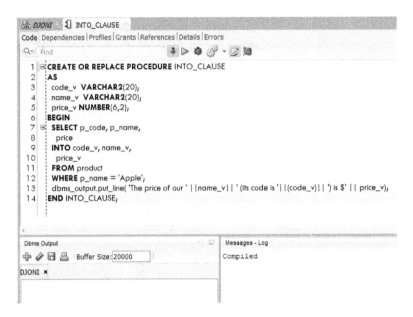

When you execute the into_clause procedure, you should see a displayed output as follows.

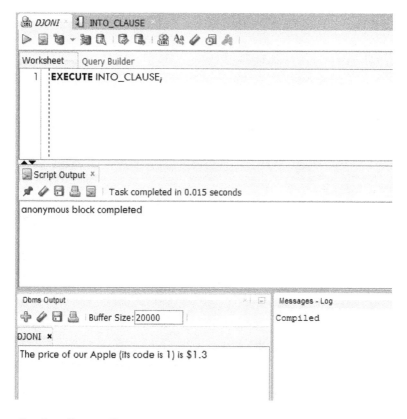

Only One Row

A SELECT INTO must return exactly one row.

In the following multiple_rows procedure, the query returns multiple rows. The procedure compiles successfully.

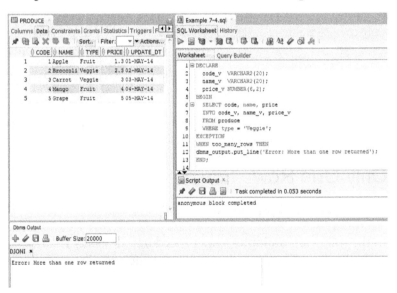

```
CREATE OR REPLACE PROCEDURE MUTIPLE_ROWS
AS
  code_v VARCHAR2(20);
  name_v VARCHAR2(20);
  price_v NUMBER(6,2);
BEGIN
  SELECT p_code, p_name, price INTO code_v, name_v, price_v FROM product;
  dbms_output.put_line( 'The price of our ' || name_v || ' (its code is '|| (code_v) || ') is $' || price_v;
END MUTIPLE_ROWS;
```

You can use the PL/SQL predefined too_many_rows exception to handle this error as shown in Example 7-4.

When you execute the multiple_rows procedure, it will fail. You will learn in Chapter 5, Exception-handling, to prevent such a failure.

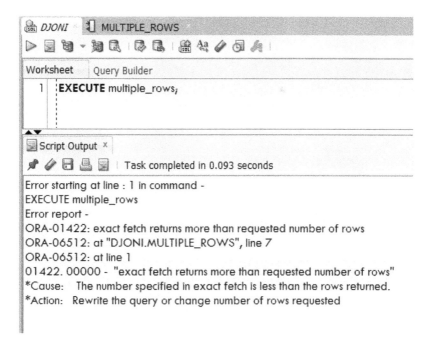

ROWTYPE and TYPE

You can use two special data types to make sure the variables you use as the INTO columns are correctly the same as the table's columns. The syntax of the ROWTYPE and TYPE datatypes syntaxes are respectively:

```
variable_name table_name%ROWTYPE;
variable_name column_name%TYPE;
```

You use ROWTYPE to at once refer to all the columns of the table; while the TYPE refers to a specific column.

The following *special_datatypes* procedure uses these two datatypes. The avg_price has the unit_price column's datatype of the produce table. The p_row consists of columns that match the product table's columns; for example, the first column, p_row.p_code has the same datatype as that of produce.code. Note the use of dot notation to refer to a column.

SELECT for UPDATE

When you need to first SELECT and then UPDATE the selected row, and you want to be sure the selected row is not updated by any other SQL statement while you are updating it, you can lock the selected row using a SELECT for UPDATE statement as demonstrated in the following *for_update* procedure.

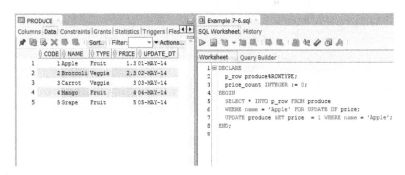

When you execute the for_update procedure, the Apple's price will be updated to 1.

Commit and Rollback

A COMMIT statement commits new, deleted and updates rows persistently in the database. You can issue a ROLLBACK statement to back out changes that have not been committed.

The following com_rb procedure has both the COMMIT and ROLLBACK statements. The update to the Apple's price is committed if it is the only product with 1.5 price (which is true); otherwise, the update is roll-backed.

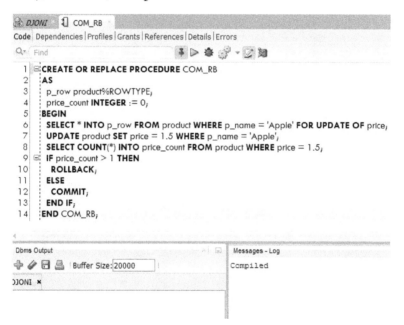

Note that a procedure can also have a DELETE statement.

Chapter 4: Cursor

A cursor is a storage of, and pointer to, the rows returned by a query. You use a cursor to access the rows one at a time sequentially.

The declaration syntax of a cursor is:

```
DECLARE
CURSOR cursor IS query;
```

In the executable part, open the cursor; fetch a row, when you are done with the cursor, close it. The syntax of the OPEN, FETCH, and CLOSE statements are respectively:

```
OPEN cursor;

FETCH cursor INTO variables;

CLOSE cursor;
```

The FETCH has an INTO clause for storing a row from the cursor into the variables. All data types of the variables must match with the data types of the columns of the rows.

In the following product_cur procedure, a cursor named *cur* is declared on line 3 – 5; its query returns all rows from the *product* table. To match the data types of the cursor's columns, the *product_rows* variable used on line 9 to store the cursor's rows is declared as the cursor's row type.

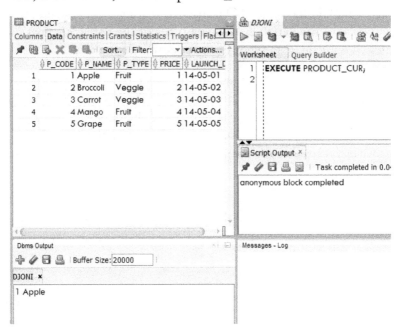

```
    DJONI      PRODUCT_CUR
Code  Dependencies | Profiles | Grants | References | Details | Errors
  Find
  1  ⊟CREATE OR REPLACE PROCEDURE PRODUCT_CUR
  2   :AS
  3   :  CURSOR cur
  4   :  IS
  5   :   SELECT * FROM product;
  6   :  product_rows cur%rowtype; -- declared having the cursor's type
  7   :BEGIN
  8   :  OPEN cur;
  9   :  FETCH cur INTO product_rows;
 10   :  dbms_output.put_line(product_rows.p_code || '' || product_rows.p_name);
 11   :END PRODUCT_CUR;

Messages - Log
Compiled
```

The program has only one FETCH, which fetches the first row, the Broccoli, from the product_rows variable.

```
  PRODUCT                                          DJONI
Columns Data Constraints | Grants | Statistics | Triggers | Fla◀▶
   Sort.. | Filter:     ▼ ▼ Actions...     Worksheet   Query Builder
    P_CODE P_NAME P_TYPE PRICE LAUNCH_D    1  EXECUTE PRODUCT_CUR;
  1      1 Apple   Fruit     1 14-05-01     2
  2      2 Broccoli Veggie   2 14-05-02
  3      3 Carrot  Veggie    3 14-05-03
  4      4 Mango   Fruit     4 14-05-04
  5      5 Grape   Fruit     5 14-05-05

                                            Script Output ×
                                            Task completed in 0.0
                                           anonymous block completed

Dbms Output                               Messages - Log
  Buffer Size: 20000
DJONI ×
1 Apple
```

Note that:

Each fetch takes one row from the cursor; to fetch more than one row you place the fetch inside a loop.

To fetch the rows in a specific order, you define the order in the cursor's query.

PL/SQL Variable in the Query

A cursor's query can include variables.

In the following variable_in_cur procedure, the cursor's query uses price_increase variable in its second output column. This column is added to the produce's unit_price; the sum is aliased as new_price.

```
PRODUCT        VARIABLE_IN_CUR
Code  Dependencies  Profiles  Grants  References  Details  Errors
Find                                                                DJONI
 1   CREATE OR REPLACE PROCEDURE VARIABLE_IN_CUR
 2   AS
 3     price_increase NUMBER(2,2) := 0.01;
 4     CURSOR cur
 5     IS
 6       SELECT price, (price + price_increase) new_price FROM product;
 7     price_rows cur%rowtype;
 8   BEGIN
 9     OPEN cur;
10     FETCH cur INTO price_rows;
11     dbms_output.put_line('The current price of ' || price_rows.price || ' will increase to ' || price_rows.new_price);
12   END VARIABLE_IN_CUR;

                                                                   12

Dbms Output                                    Messages - Log
    Buffer Size: 20000                         Compiled
DJONI  x
```

When you execute the variable_in_cur procedure you will see the following.

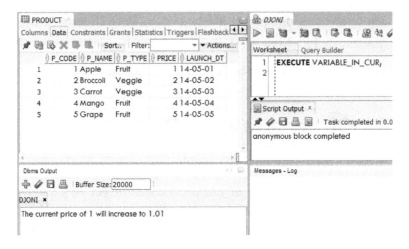

Cursor Attributes

PL/SQL provides %ISOPEN, %FOUND,%NOTFOUND, and %ROWCOUNT attributes.

As you will not generally know in advance the number of rows in a cursor, you don't know when to stop the loop iteration. Fortunately you can use the %notfound cursor attribute to detect when there is no more row in a cursor. In the following not_found procedure, the "EXIT WHEN %notfound" statement stops the loop from fetching further beyond the last row.

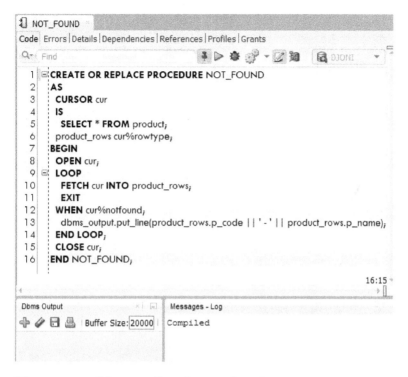

The output of the not_found procedure is as seen next.

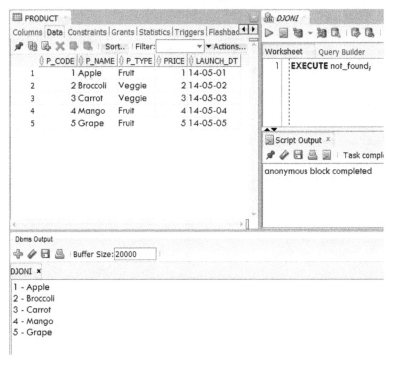

The use of the %isopen attribute is demonstrated in the following is_open procedure. The cur cursor queries the name column from the produce table and stores it into name_c variable. As the name_c variable is too short to store the name, a run_time exception occurs. The exception is handled by the WHEN OTHERS. Line 13 uses the %isopen to check the status of the c cursor and finds that the cursor is still open, hence it is closed.

Note that the dbms_output.put_line can only display string. As %isopen has a Boolean datatype, we use the s variable to store the string message conveying the cursor open status that we want to display.

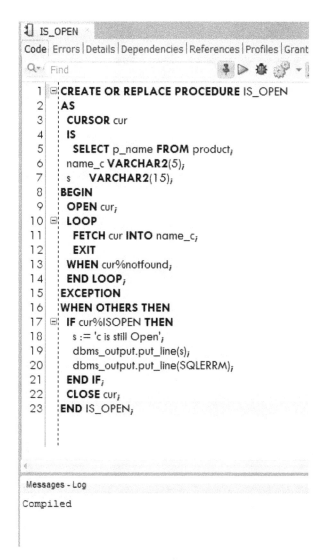

```
1  CREATE OR REPLACE PROCEDURE IS_OPEN
2  AS
3    CURSOR cur
4    IS
5      SELECT p_name FROM product;
6    name_c VARCHAR2(5);
7    s    VARCHAR2(15);
8  BEGIN
9    OPEN cur;
10   LOOP
11     FETCH cur INTO name_c;
12     EXIT
13   WHEN cur%notfound;
14   END LOOP;
15   EXCEPTION
16   WHEN OTHERS THEN
17     IF cur%ISOPEN THEN
18       s := 'c is still Open';
19       dbms_output.put_line(s);
20       dbms_output.put_line(SQLERRM);
21     END IF;
22     CLOSE cur;
23   END IS_OPEN;
```

Messages - Log

Compiled

When you execute the is_open procedure, you will get an error message.

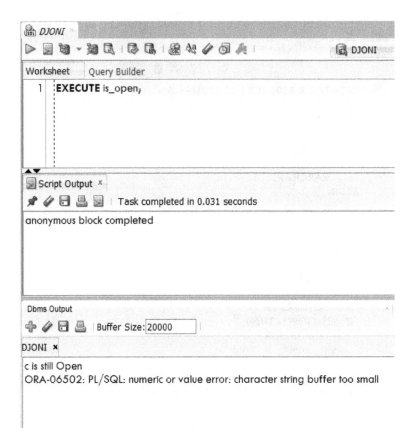

Cursor Last Row

Fetching beyond the last row does not produce any error, the value in the INTO variable is still that from last rows fetched.

The following last_row procedure will be completed successfully. The loop iterates six times. As the product table has five rows only and code 5 is the last code fetched, the 5th and the 6th outputs are 5.

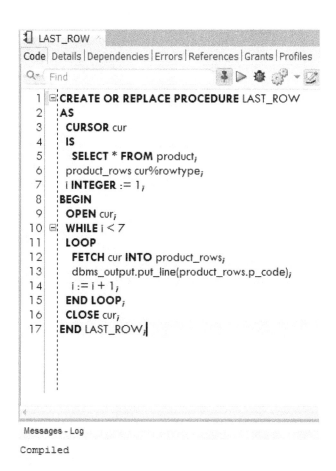

```
    LAST_ROW
  Code  Details | Dependencies | Errors | References | Grants | Profiles
  Q    Find

 1   CREATE OR REPLACE PROCEDURE LAST_ROW
 2   AS
 3     CURSOR cur
 4     IS
 5      SELECT * FROM product;
 6     product_rows cur%rowtype;
 7     i INTEGER := 1;
 8   BEGIN
 9     OPEN cur;
10     WHILE i < 7
11     LOOP
12       FETCH cur INTO product_rows;
13       dbms_output.put_line(product_rows.p_code);
14       i := i + 1;
15     END LOOP;
16     CLOSE cur;
17   END LAST_ROW;
```

Messages - Log

Compiled

Here is the output from the last_row procedure.

Cursor FOR Loop

The cursor FOR loop specifies a sequence of statements to be repeated once for each row returned by a cursor. Use the cursor FOR loop if you need to process every record from a cursor; it does not need you to open, fetch and close the cursor.

The following cursor_loop procedure, using the cur_index (a variable that you don't need to declare), the for-loop on line 7 – 10 displays the code and name of every product from the cursor.

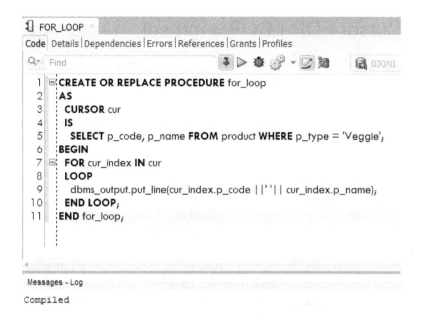

You will see the following output.

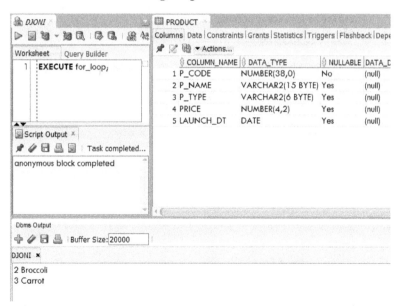

Cursor FOR LOOP short cut

A statement with the following syntax effectively loops through the rows returned by the query.

```
FOR returned_rows IN
(query)
LOOP
   statements;
END LOOP;
```

No cursor is declared. You don't need to declare the returned_rows which stores the query's returned rows. The loop iterates through all rows returned by the query.

In the following short_cut procedure all rows from the product table are returned. These rows are all processed one by one sequentially. The product's type and name will be displayed.

```
1  CREATE OR REPLACE PROCEDURE short_cut
2  AS
3    output VARCHAR2(40);
4  BEGIN
5    FOR product_rows IN
6    (SELECT * FROM product
7    )
8    LOOP
9      output := 'The name of this ' || product_rows.p_type || ' is: ' || product_rows.p_name;
10     dbms_output.put_line(output);
11   END LOOP;
12  END short_cut;
```

```
Messages - Log
Compiled
```

Here is the output from the short_cut procedure.

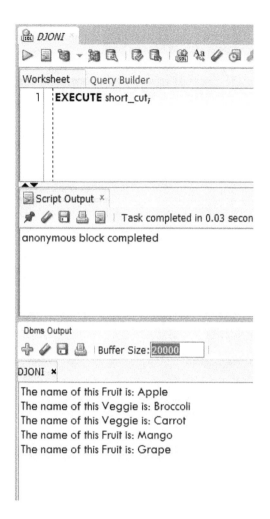

View

So far, the queries of our cursors are on tables. The query of a cursor can also be on a view.

Assume we have a view, product_view, created using the CREATE VIEW statement as follows.

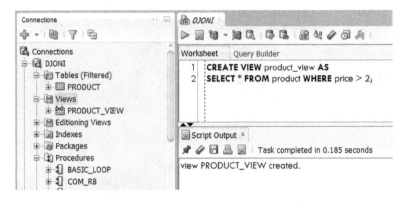

The following view_cursor has a query that uses the product_view view you have just created.

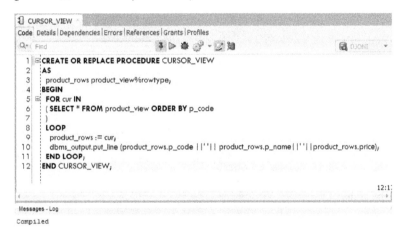

Here is the output.

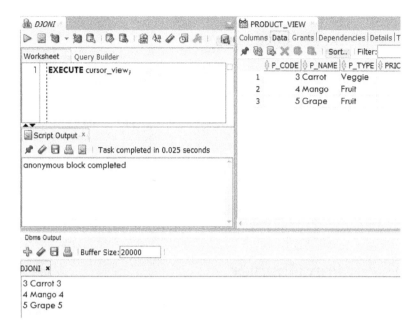

Chapter 5: Exception-handling

If a procedure runs into a problem, it will abort; the program fails at run-time.

The following no_row procedure fails because the query does not return any row; the product table does not have any Pineapple.

The program is aborted; you will see an error message saying "no data found".

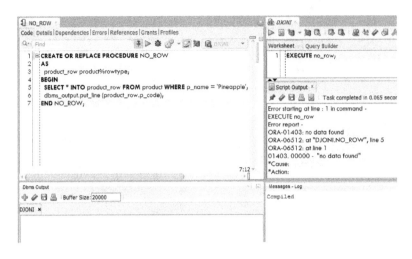

Exception Handler

You can prevent a procedure run-time failure using an exception handler.

The syntax of an exception handler statement is:

WHEN exception THEN exception-handler statements

In the following no_data_found procedure, a no_data_found exception is handled. When the exception occurs, the dbm_output.put_line is executed; the procedure gets completed successfully.

Multiple Exception-handling Statement

An Exception part can have more than one statement.

The multi_handler procedure has **two** exception statements. Any error that is not too_many_rows is handled by the OTHERS statement. The error encounters by this program is caused by the query that does not return any row, hence this error is handled by the OTHERS handler. (The OTHERS exception is used for catch-all other types of error not caught by other specific exception handlers.)

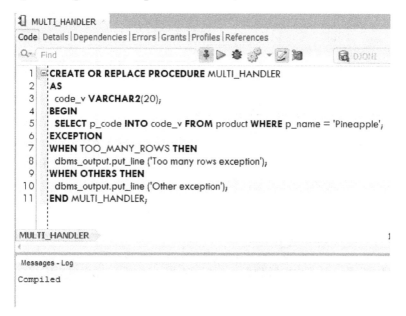

Here is the output.

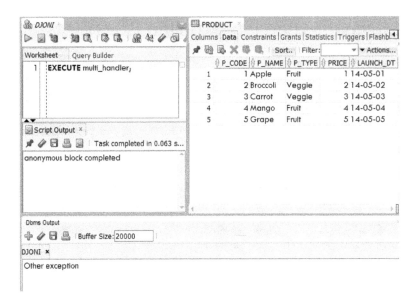

Combining Exceptions

If you want the same exception action for different exception-handlers, you can put them into one exception. The syntax is then as follows.

WHEN exception1 OR exception2 OR...

THEN exception_action

The following combined_exception has one exception with two handlers.

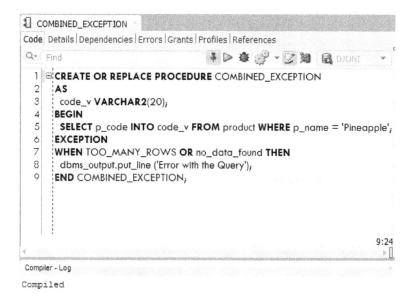

The output of the combined_exception is as follows.

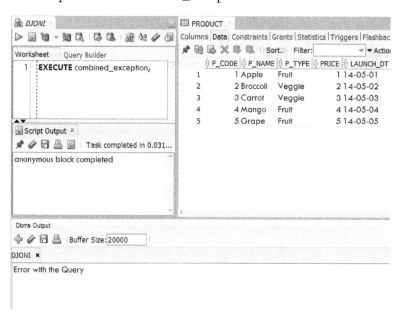

Predefined Exceptions

NO_DATA_FOUND and OTHERS that we already used are two of the PL/SQL predefined exceptions.

VALUE_ERROR is another example of predefined exception as used in the following value_error procedure. Line 5 tries to assign a string of six characters, which is longer than the maximum length specified for the x variable. The VALUE_ERROR exception handler on line 7 - 9 catches this error.

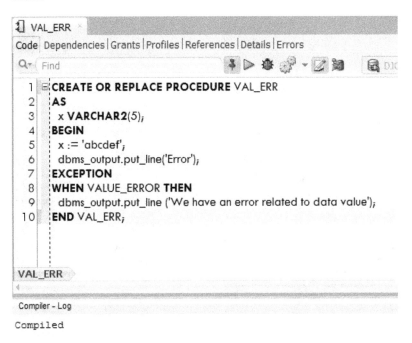

```
1  CREATE OR REPLACE PROCEDURE VAL_ERR
2  AS
3    x VARCHAR2(5);
4  BEGIN
5    x := 'abcdef';
6    dbms_output.put_line('Error');
7  EXCEPTION
8  WHEN VALUE_ERROR THEN
9    dbms_output.put_line ('We have an error related to data value');
10 END VAL_ERR;
```

Compiler - Log

Compiled

When you execute the val_err procedure you will see the followig:

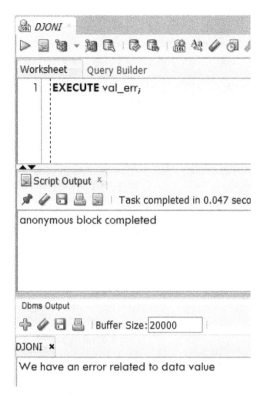

Please consult the Oracle PL/SQL manual for a complete list of the predefined exceptions.

SQLCODE and SQLERRM functions

PL/SQL provides SQLCODE and SQLERRM functions; when you call these functions, they will return the Oracle error code and message respectively for the error encountered by your program at run time.

The following example code_msg procedure demonstrates the use of the two functions on line 7 and 8.

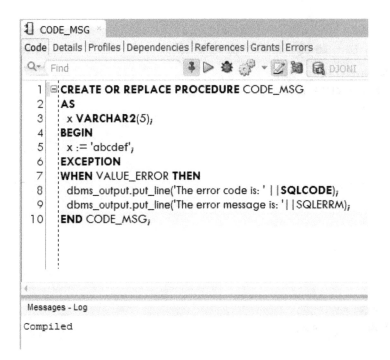

```
CREATE OR REPLACE PROCEDURE CODE_MSG
AS
  x VARCHAR2(5);
BEGIN
  x := 'abcdef';
EXCEPTION
WHEN VALUE_ERROR THEN
  dbms_output.put_line('The error code is: ' || SQLCODE);
  dbms_output.put_line('The error message is: ' || SQLERRM);
END CODE_MSG;
```

Messages - Log

Compiled

Here is the output.

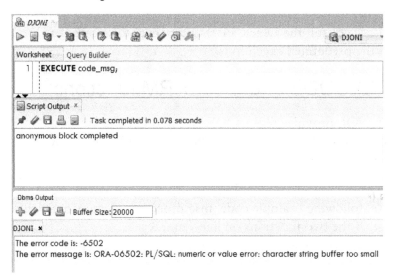

```
EXECUTE code_msg;
```

Script Output ×

Task completed in 0.078 seconds

anonymous block completed

Dbms Output

Buffer Size: 20000

DJONI ×

The error code is: -6502
The error message is: ORA-06502: PL/SQL: numeric or value error: character string buffer too small

Defining Oracle Error

You might have an error that does not have a pre-defined exception. Fortunately, PL/SQL has a a solution, a feature known as PRAGMA EXCEPTION_INIT. You first declare an EXCEPTION in the Declaration part; its syntax is as follows.

```
exception EXCEPTION;
```

Then, also in the Declaration part, you define that exception with the following syntax.

```
PRAGMA EXCEPTION_INIT(exception, -
    Oracle_error_number);
```

where `exception_name` is the name of the exception you already declare, and the number is a negative value corresponding to an `ORA-` error number. You will need to find out this error number in the Oracle manual, or find it using the SQLCODE function we discussed earlier and shown on the code_msg procedure.

In the following exc_init procedure the UPDATE tries to update a primary key to an existing value causing an exception. The error number for violating unique constraint violation is -1.

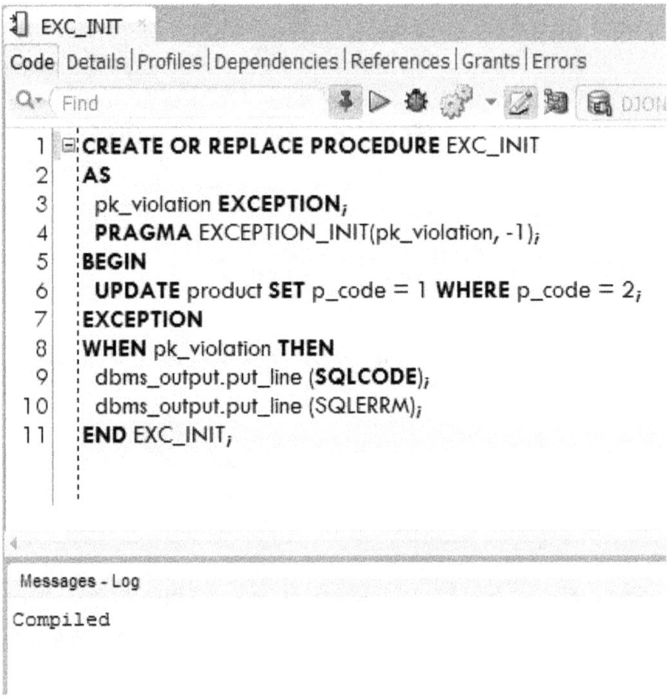

```
 1  CREATE OR REPLACE PROCEDURE EXC_INIT
 2  AS
 3    pk_violation EXCEPTION;
 4    PRAGMA EXCEPTION_INIT(pk_violation, -1);
 5  BEGIN
 6    UPDATE product SET p_code = 1 WHERE p_code = 2;
 7  EXCEPTION
 8  WHEN pk_violation THEN
 9    dbms_output.put_line (SQLCODE);
10    dbms_output.put_line (SQLERRM);
11  END EXC_INIT;
```

Messages - Log

Compiled

Executing the exc_init procedure, you will see the following:

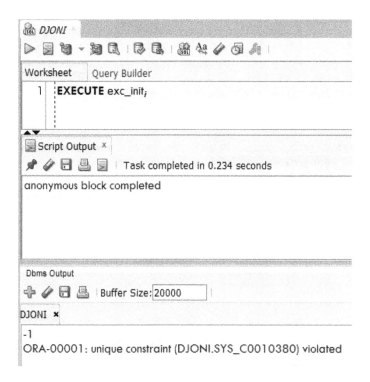

User Defined Exception

All previous exceptions were run-time errors. You can also define your own exceptions that are not run-time errors. Your handler will take care of your pre-defined exceptions in the same fashion as run-time error exception-handler.

In the following user_exc procedure, we want any price higher than 4.5 treated as an exception; hence we declare it on line 4. We then use it within the IF THEN statement in on line 7 – 9 as the target of a RAISE statement (RAISE is a reserved word). The Exception part must have a handler for the exception as shown on line 11 – 12.

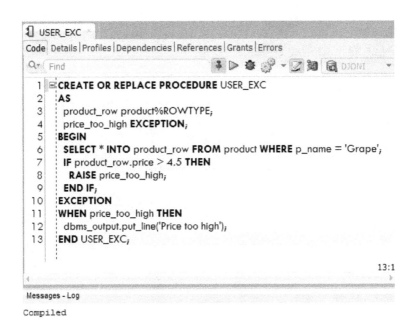

You will see the output as follows.

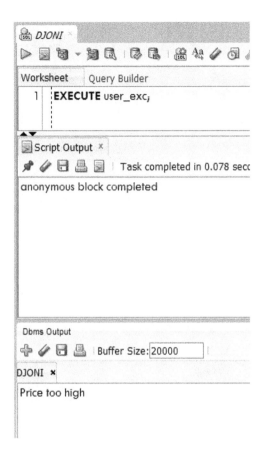

Chapter 6: Creating Stored Function

If a procedure runs into a problem, it will abort; the program fails at run-time.

The following no_row procedure fails because the query does not return any row; the product table does not have any Pineapple.

The program is aborted; you will see an error message saying "no data found".

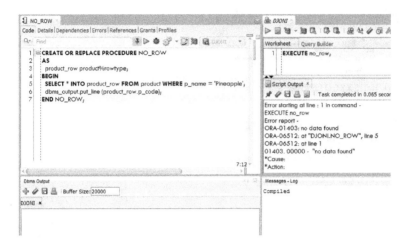

Exception Handler

You can prevent a procedure run-time failure using an exception handler.

The syntax of an exception handler statement is:

WHEN exception THEN exception-handler statements

In the following no_data_found procedure, a no_data_found exception is handled. When the exception occurs, the dbm_output.put_line is executed; the procedure gets completed successfully.

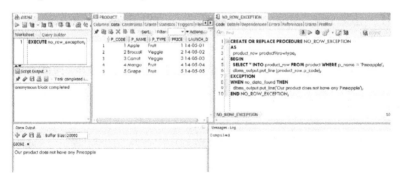

Multiple Exception-handling Statement

An Exception part can have more than one statement.

The multi_handler procedure has **two** exception statements. Any error that is not too_many_rows is handled by the OTHERS statement. The error encounters by this program is caused by the query that does not return any row, hence this error is handled by the OTHERS handler. (The OTHERS exception is used for catch-all other types of error not caught by other specific exception handlers.)

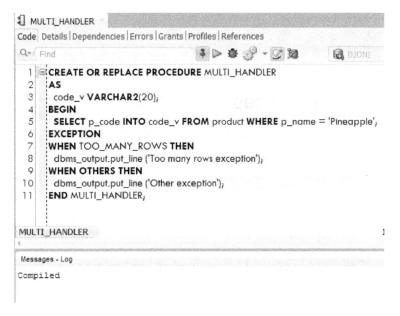

Here is the output.

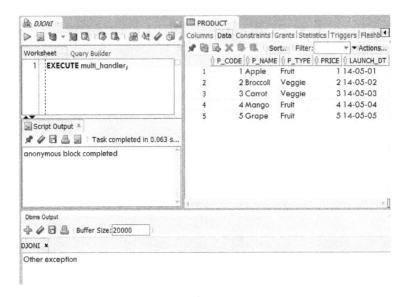

Combining Exceptions

If you want the same exception action for different exception-handlers, you can put them into one exception. The syntax is then as follows.

WHEN exception1 OR exception2 OR…

THEN exception_action

The following combined_exception has one exception with two handlers.

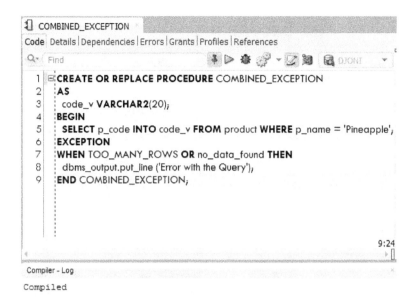

```
1   CREATE OR REPLACE PROCEDURE COMBINED_EXCEPTION
2   AS
3     code_v VARCHAR2(20);
4   BEGIN
5     SELECT p_code INTO code_v FROM product WHERE p_name = 'Pineapple';
6   EXCEPTION
7   WHEN TOO_MANY_ROWS OR no_data_found THEN
8     dbms_output.put_line ('Error with the Query');
9   END COMBINED_EXCEPTION;
```

Compiler - Log

Compiled

The output of the combined_exception is as follows.

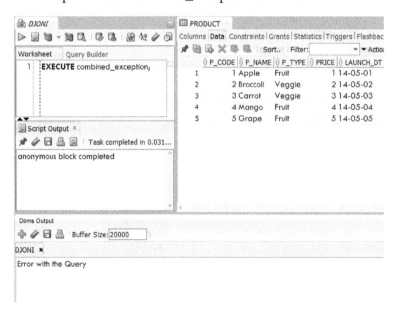

Predefined Exceptions

NO_DATA_FOUND and OTHERS that we already used are two of the PL/SQL predefined exceptions.

VALUE_ERROR is another example of predefined exception as used in the following value_error procedure. Line 5 tries to assign a string of six characters, which is longer than the maximum length specified for the x variable. The VALUE_ERROR exception handler on line 7 - 9 catches this error.

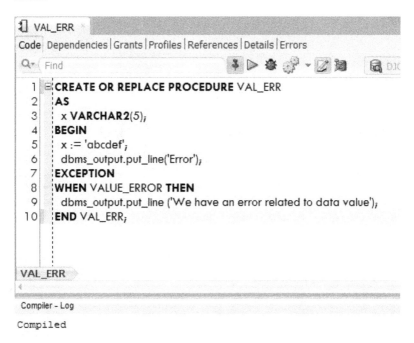

When you execute the val_err procedure you will see the followig:

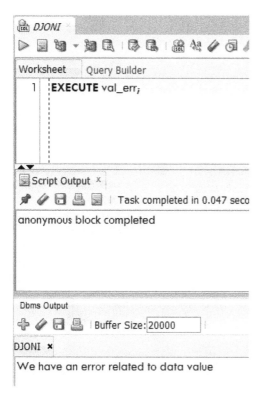

Please consult the Oracle PL/SQL manual for a complete list of the predefined exceptions.

SQLCODE and SQLERRM functions

PL/SQL provides SQLCODE and SQLERRM functions; when you call these functions, they will return the Oracle error code and message respectively for the error encountered by your program at run time.

The following example code_msg procedure demonstrates the use of the two functions on line 7 and 8.

```
CODE_MSG
Code Details Profiles Dependencies References Grants Errors
Q  Find                          DJONI

 1  CREATE OR REPLACE PROCEDURE CODE_MSG
 2  AS
 3    x VARCHAR2(5);
 4  BEGIN
 5    x := 'abcdef';
 6  EXCEPTION
 7  WHEN VALUE_ERROR THEN
 8    dbms_output.put_line('The error code is: ' ||SQLCODE);
 9    dbms_output.put_line('The error message is: '||SQLERRM);
10  END CODE_MSG;

Messages - Log
Compiled
```

Here is the output.

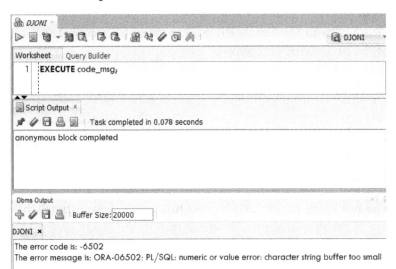

```
DJONI
                                          DJONI
Worksheet   Query Builder
 1  EXECUTE code_msg;

Script Output ×
   Task completed in 0.078 seconds
anonymous block completed

Dbms Output
   Buffer Size: 20000
DJONI ×
The error code is: -6502
The error message is: ORA-06502: PL/SQL: numeric or value error: character string buffer too small
```

Defining Oracle Error

You might have an error that does not have a pre-defined exception. Fortunately, PL/SQL has a a solution, a feature known as PRAGMA EXCEPTION_INIT. You first declare an EXCEPTION in the Declaration part; its syntax is as follows.

```
exception EXCEPTION;
```

Then, also in the Declaration part, you define that exception with the following syntax.

```
PRAGMA EXCEPTION_INIT(exception, -
     Oracle_error_number);
```

where `exception_name` is the name of the exception you already declare, and the number is a negative value corresponding to an `ORA-` error number. You will need to find out this error number in the Oracle manual, or find it using the SQLCODE function we discussed earlier and shown on the code_msg procedure.

In the following exc_init procedure the UPDATE tries to update a primary key to an existing value causing an exception. The error number for violating unique constraint violation is -1.

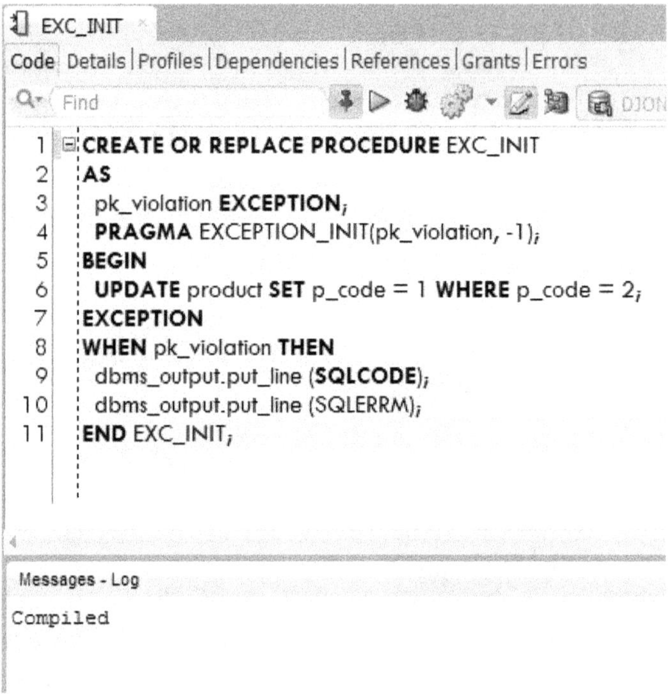

EXC_INIT

Code Details | Profiles | Dependencies | References | Grants | Errors

Q Find

```
 1  CREATE OR REPLACE PROCEDURE EXC_INIT
 2  AS
 3    pk_violation EXCEPTION;
 4    PRAGMA EXCEPTION_INIT(pk_violation, -1);
 5  BEGIN
 6    UPDATE product SET p_code = 1 WHERE p_code = 2;
 7  EXCEPTION
 8  WHEN pk_violation THEN
 9    dbms_output.put_line (SQLCODE);
10    dbms_output.put_line (SQLERRM);
11  END EXC_INIT;
```

Messages - Log

Compiled

Executing the exc_init procedure, you will see the following:

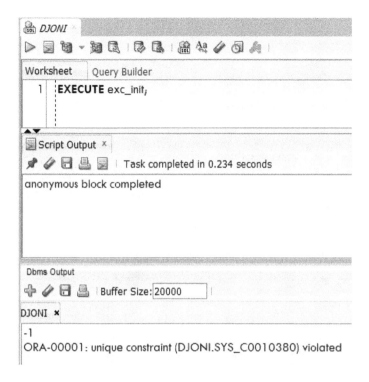

User Defined Exception

All previous exceptions were run-time errors. You can also define your own exceptions that are not run-time errors. Your handler will take care of your pre-defined exceptions in the same fashion as run-time error exception-handler.

In the following user_exc procedure, we want any price higher than 4.5 treated as an exception; hence we declare it on line 4. We then use it within the IF THEN statement in on line 7 – 9 as the target of a RAISE statement (RAISE is a reserved word). The Exception part must have a handler for the exception as shown on line 11 – 12.

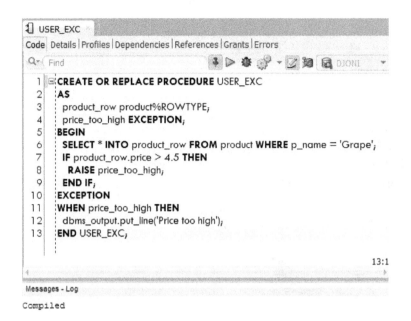

You will see the output as follows.

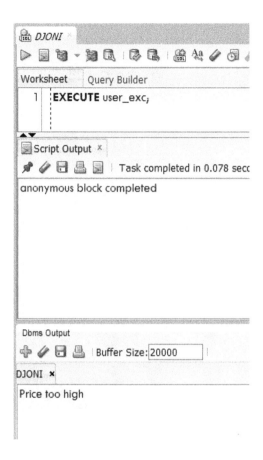

Chapter 7: Package

We can put together procedures and functions into a stored package. The dbms_output.put_line procedure we have been using is one of the built-in packages. Put_line is one of the procedures in the dbms_output package. We access the procedures and function in a package using a dot notation.

A package has two parts: specification and body. The specification declares the procedures and functions in the body.

Creating Package

To create the specification right click the package folder and select New Package.

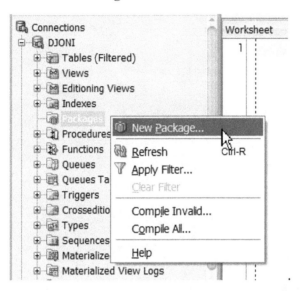

Edit the name and click OK.

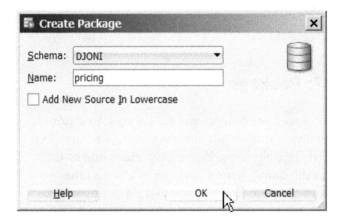

Replace the /* TODO ... */ comment with the procedure and function declarations you want to include in the package.

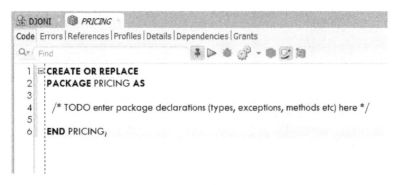

Here is the package now with our price-related procedures (increase_price and increase_10pct) and a function (new_price). You need to compile the package.

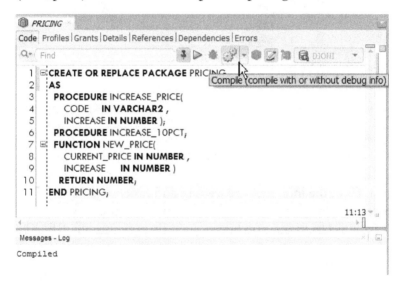

Next, you need to create the body. Right click the package and select Create Body.

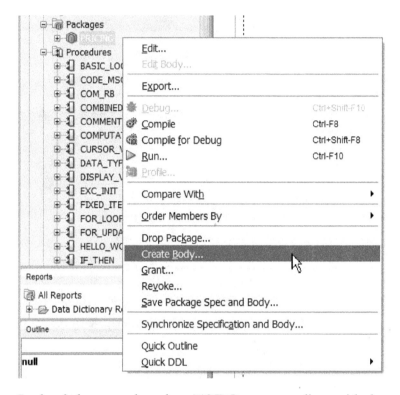

In the skeleton, replace the --TODO comment lines with the respective procedures and function (you can copy and paste them from the individual procedure and function). As increase_10pct procedure and new_price function have variable declarations, you have to add them before the BEGIN keyword.

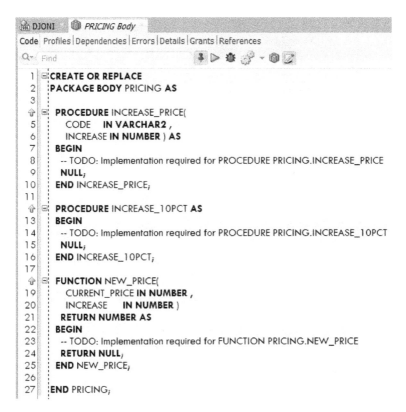

The pricing body should look like the following. You can now compile it.

```
 1  CREATE OR REPLACE PACKAGE BODY PRICING
 2  AS
 3  PROCEDURE INCREASE_PRICE(
 4      CODE    IN VARCHAR2 ,
 5      INCREASE IN NUMBER )
 6  AS
 7  BEGIN
 8    UPDATE product SET price = price + (price * increase/100) WHERE p_code = code;
 9    NULL;
10  END INCREASE_PRICE;
11  PROCEDURE INCREASE_10PCT
12  AS
13    avg_price NUMBER;
14  BEGIN
15    SELECT AVG(price) INTO avg_price FROM product;
16    dbms_output.put_line('The average price is: ' || avg_price);
17    UPDATE product SET price = price + 0.1 * avg_price WHERE price < avg_price;
18  END INCREASE_10PCT;
19  FUNCTION NEW_PRICE(
20      CURRENT_PRICE IN NUMBER ,
21      INCREASE     IN NUMBER )
22    RETURN NUMBER
23  AS
24    new_price NUMBER(8,2);
25  BEGIN
26    new_price := current_price + (current_price * increase);
27    RETURN new_price;
28  END NEW_PRICE;
29  END PRICING;
```

Using Package

To refer a procedure or function in a package, you need to use the dot notation; for example, **pricing.increase_price**

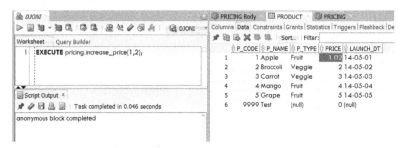

User Interface

The specifiction of a package acts as an interface to the package users. A change of implementation in the body is transparent to the users.

Let's say there is a change on the name of the price column of the product table. The column name is unit_price.

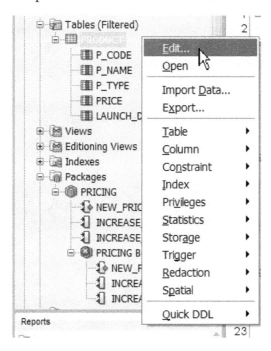

Edit the colum name, then click OK.

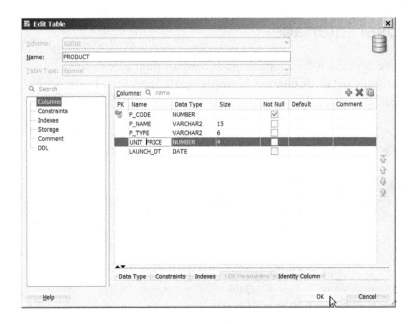

The column name change impacts the body of our pricing package. Hence, we need to adjust it accordingly.

Right click the PRICING body and select Edit.

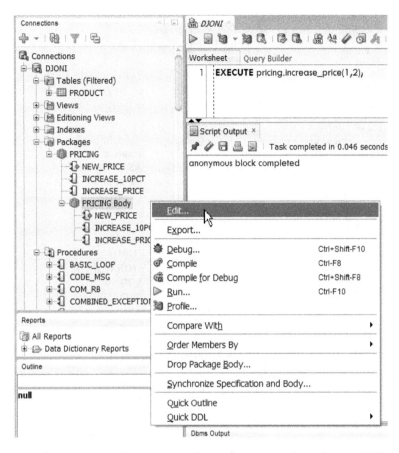

We change the column name from price to unit_price by Edit and Replace.

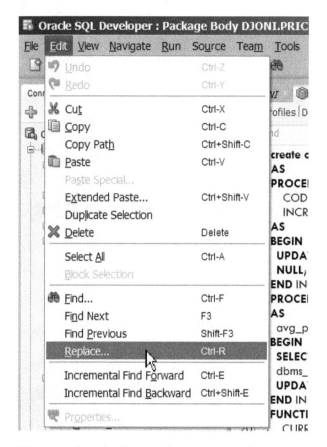

Then, replace it all over the source code.

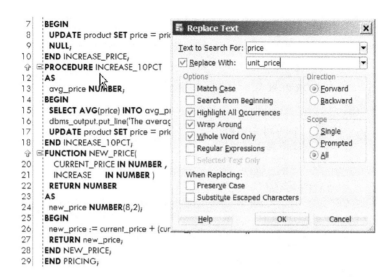

```
 7  BEGIN
 8    UPDATE product SET price = pri
 9    NULL;
10  END INCREASE_PRICE;
    PROCEDURE INCREASE_10PCT
12  AS
13    avg_price NUMBER;
14  BEGIN
15    SELECT AVG(price) INTO avg_pr
16    dbms_output.put_line('The averaç
17    UPDATE product SET price = pri
18  END INCREASE_10PCT;
    FUNCTION NEW_PRICE(
20    CURRENT_PRICE IN NUMBER ,
21    INCREASE    IN NUMBER )
22  RETURN NUMBER
23  AS
24    new_price NUMBER(8,2);
25  BEGIN
26    new_price := current_price + (cur
27    RETURN new_price;
28  END NEW_PRICE;
29  END PRICING;
```

Replace Text dialog:

Text to Search For: price

☑ Replace With: unit_price

Options
- [ ] Match Case
- [ ] Search from Beginning
- [x] Highlight All Occurrences
- [x] Wrap Around
- [x] Whole Word Only
- [ ] Regular Expressions
- [ ] Selected Text Only

When Replacing:
- [ ] Preserve Case
- [ ] Substitute Escaped Characters

Direction
- (•) Forward
- ( ) Backward

Scope
- ( ) Single
- ( ) Prompted
- (•) All

Help   OK   Cancel

Our package body will now look like the following. Compile it, and the users can then use any of procedure and function, just like there has been no change.

```
 1  CREATE OR REPLACE PACKAGE BODY PRICING
 2  AS
    PROCEDURE INCREASE_PRICE(
 4      CODE   IN VARCHAR2 ,
 5      INCREASE IN NUMBER )
 6  AS
 7  BEGIN
 8    UPDATE product
 9    SET unit_price = unit_price + (unit_price * increase/100)
10    WHERE p_code  = code;
11    NULL;
12  END INCREASE_PRICE;
    PROCEDURE INCREASE_10PCT
14  AS
15    avg_price NUMBER;
16  BEGIN
17    SELECT AVG(unit_price) INTO avg_price FROM product;
18    dbms_output.put_line('The average unit_price is: ' || avg_price);
19    UPDATE product
20    SET unit_price   = unit_price + 0.1 * avg_price
21    WHERE unit_price < avg_price;
22  END INCREASE_10PCT;
    FUNCTION NEW_PRICE(
24      CURRENT_PRICE IN NUMBER ,
25      INCREASE     IN NUMBER )
26    RETURN NUMBER
27  AS
28    new_price NUMBER(8,2);
29  BEGIN
30    new_price := current_price + (current_price * increase);
31    RETURN new_price;
32  END NEW_PRICE;
33  END PRICING;
```

Chapter 8: Permission

You can let others use your procedure, function, or package by granting them permission using the GRANT statement.

Granting hello_world to Fred

To grant our hello_world procedure, for example, right click the procedure and select Grant.

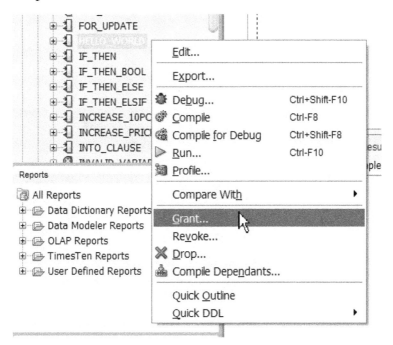

Select the user or role from the drop down list, for example, FRED.

Then select EXECUTE to allow FRED to execute the hello_world procedure.

Next, click the Apply button.

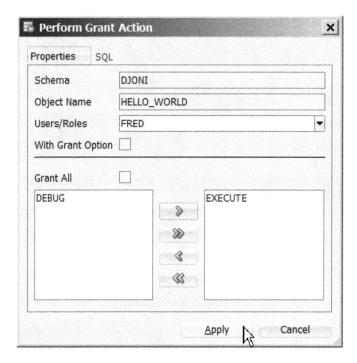

Finally, click OK.

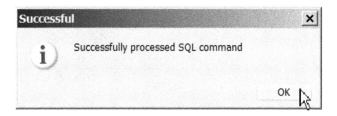

To test if FRED has the execution right on the hello_world procedure, connect as FRED.

You will need to create user FRED and allow him to create a connection (authorize him to CREATE SESSION).

Then, execute the procedure. Don't forget the set the Dbms Output pane for FRED.

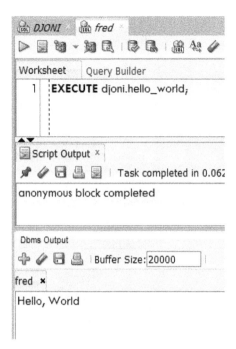

Granting to Public

Instead of specific user or role, you can grant to everybody by selecting PUBLIC from the drop-down list on the Perform Grant Action.

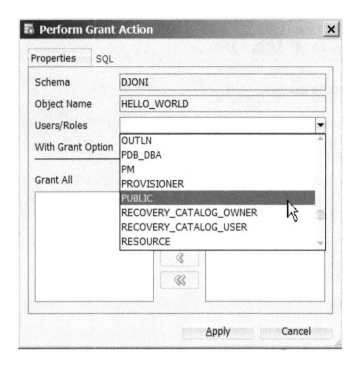

Invoker's Right

You can add an AUTHID clause on the CREATE PROCECURE to control the access to the object used by the procedure.

```
CREATE PROCEDURE procedure_name AUTHID definer or
    current_user
AS ...
```

The default is AUTHID definer (without specifying the AUTHID clause), which means when the procedure is executed, all access to the objects used by the procedure borrows your privileges of the objects. On the other hand, if you specify AUTHID current_user, the user executing the procedure must have his own privilege to access the objects.

Assume you already grant Fred, he will successfully execute the sql_statement procedure though he does not have access to the product table.

Here are the sql_statement procedure and product table before he executes the procedure.

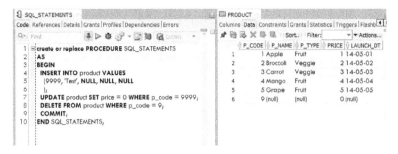

He will successfully executes the procedure and the product table is effected correctly. Note that you must specify your schema (DJONI in my case) using the dot notation (DJONI.SQL_STATEMENTS).

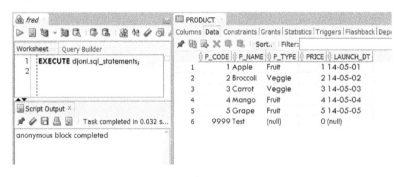

He was able to execute the procedure successfully using your privilege, though he himself does not have access to the product table.

Let's now change the AUTHID on the procedure to current_user. Don't forget to re-compile.

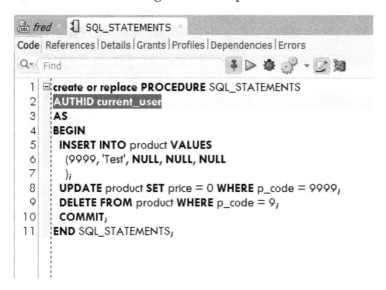

Now, when Fred executes the procedure, it will fail.

Note that you can apply the same invoker's right to functions and packages.

Appendix A: Installing Oracle Database XE

Go to
http://www.oracle.com/technetwork/indexes/downloads/ind
ex.html

Locate and download the Windows version of the Oracle
Database Express Edition (XE). You will be requested to
accept the license agreement. If you don't have one, create an
account; it's free.

Unzip the downloaded file to a folder in your local drive, and
then, double-click the setup.exe file.

You will see the Welcome window.

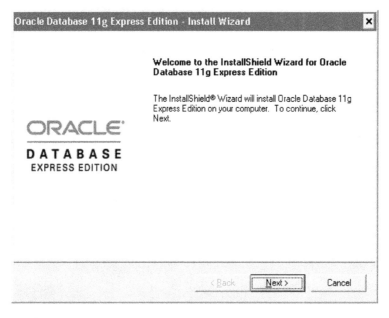

Click the Next> button, accept the agreement on the License
Agreement window, and then click the Next> button again.

The next window is the "Choose Destination Location"
window.

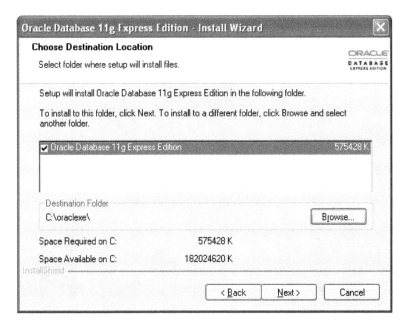

Accept the destination folder shown, or click the Browse button to choose a different folder for your installation, and then click the Next> button.

On the prompt for port numbers, accept the defaults, and then click the Next> button.

On the Passwords window, enter a password of your choice and confirm it, and then click the Next> button. The SYS and SYSTEM accounts created during this installation are for the database operation and administration, respectively. Note the password; you will use the SYSTEM account and its password for creating your own account, which you use for trying the examples.

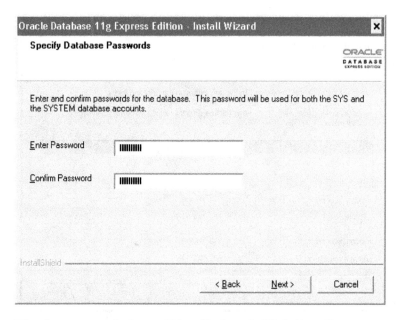

The Summary window will be displayed. Click Install.

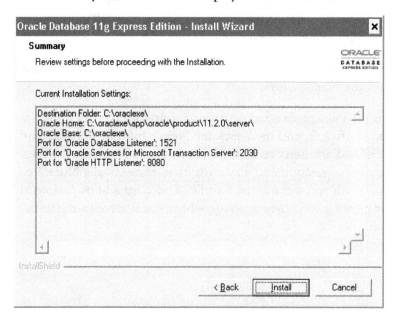

Finally, when the Installation Completion window appears, click the Finish button.

Your Oracle Database XE is now installed.

Installing SQL Developer

Go to
http://www.oracle.com/technetwork/indexes/downloads/ind
ex.html

Locate and download the SQL Developer. You will be
requested to accept the license agreement. If you don't have
one, create an account; it's free.

Unzip the downloaded file to a folder of your preference. Note
the folder name and its location; you will need to know them
to start your SQL Developer.

When the unzipping is completed, look for the
sqldeveloper.exe file.

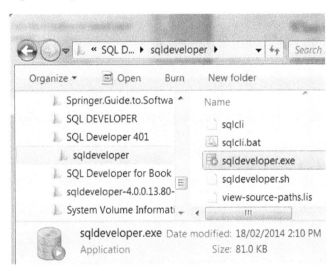

You start SQL Developer by opening (double-clicking) this
file. You might want to create a short-cut on your desktop.

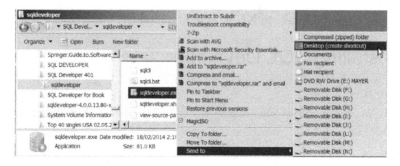

You can then start your SQL Developer by double-clicking the short-cut.

Your initial screen should look like the following. If you don't want to see the Start Page tab the next time you start SQL Developer, un-check the *Show on Startup* box at the bottom left side of the screen.

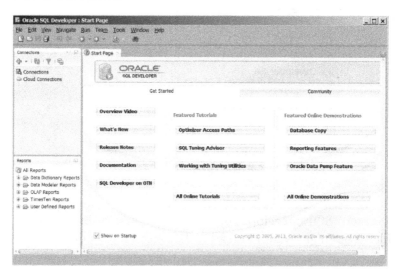

For now, close the Start Page tab by clicking its x.

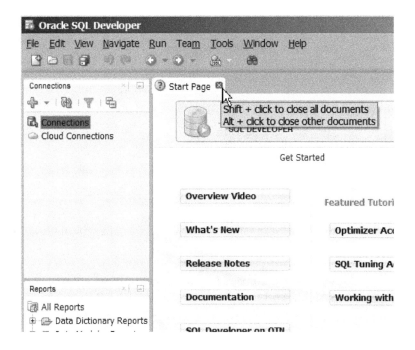

Creating Connection

To work with a database from SQL Developer, you need to have a connection.

A connection is specific to an account. As we will use the SYSTEM account to create your own account, you first have to create a connection for the SYSTEM account.

To create a connection, right-click the Connection folder.

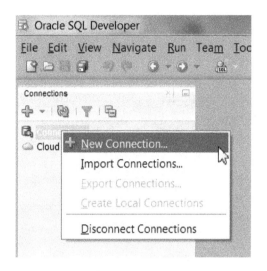

On the New/Select Database Connection window, enter a Connection Name and Username as shown. The Password is the password of SYSTEM account you entered during the Oracle database installation. Check the Save Password box.

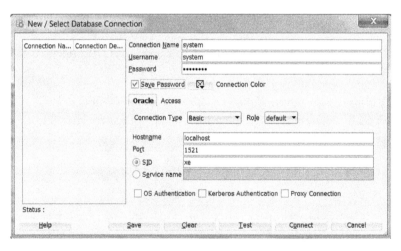

When you click the Connect button, the *system* connection you have just created should be available on the Connection Navigator.

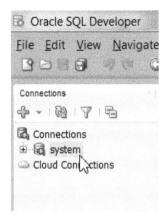

A Worksheet is opened for the system connection. The Worksheet is where you type in source codes.

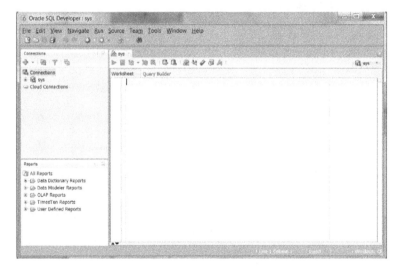

Creating Database Account

You will use your own database account (user) to try the book examples.

To create a new account, expand the system connection and locate the Other Users folder at the bottom of the folder tree.

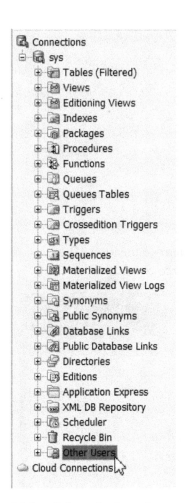

Right click and select Create User.

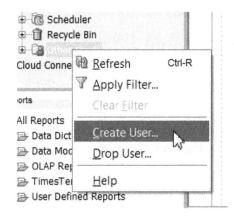

Enter a User Name of your choice, a password and its confirmation, and then click the Apply button. You should get a successful pop-up window; close it.

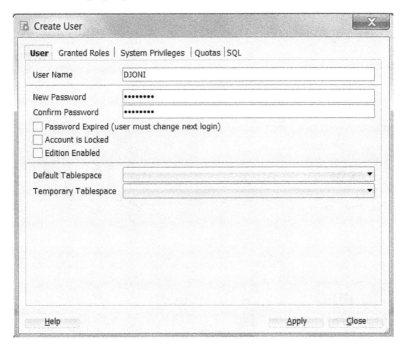

On the Granted Roles tab, click Grant All, Admin All and Default All buttons; then click the Apply button. Close the successful window and the Edit User as well.

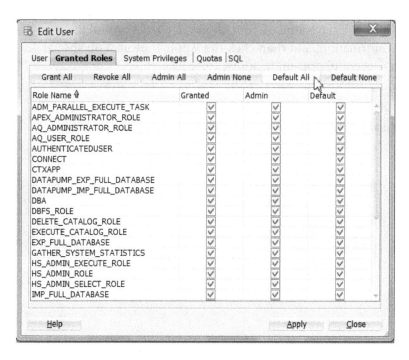

Creating Your Connection

Similar to when you created system connection earlier, now create a connection for your account.

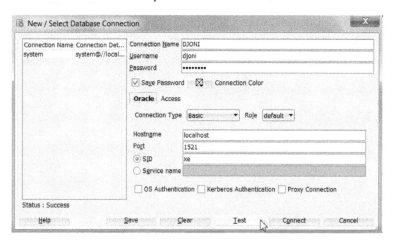

Click the Connect button. A worksheet for your connection is opened (which is *DJONI* in my case).

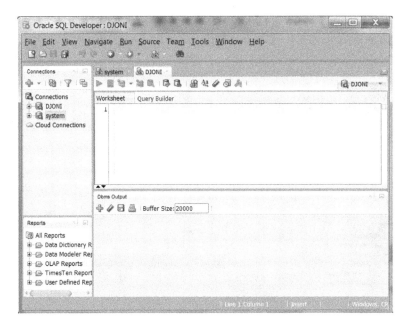

Showing Line Numbers

In describing the book examples I sometimes refer to the line numbers of the program; these are line numbers on the worksheet. To show line numbers, click Preferences from the Tools menu.

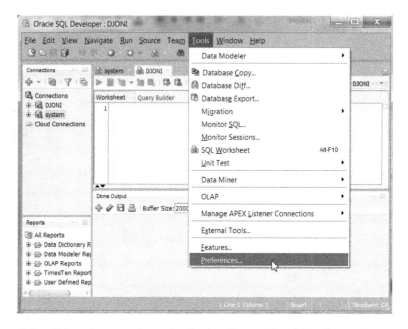

Select Line Gutter, then check the Show Line Numbers. Your Preferences should look like the following. Click the OK button.

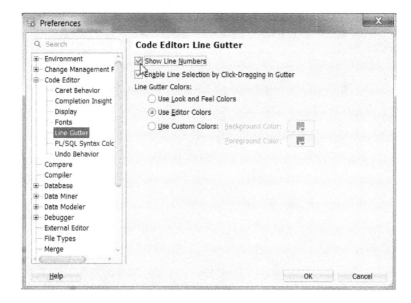

Deleting the *system* Connection

Delete the *system* connection, making sure you don't use this account mistakenly. Click Yes when you are prompted to confirm the deletion. Your SQL Developer is now set.

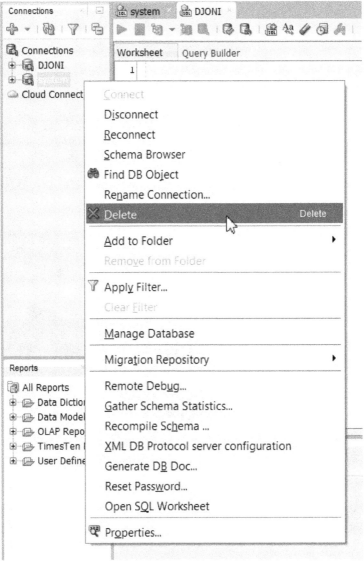

Close the *system* worksheet.

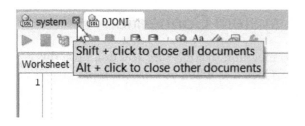

Using SQL Developer

This chapter shows you how to use the SQL Developer features that you will use to try the book examples.

Entering SQL statement and PL/SQL source code

The worksheet is where you enter SQL statement and PL/SQL source code.

Start your SQL Developer if you have not done so. To open a worksheet for your connection, click the + (folder expansion) or double-click the connection name. Alternatively, right-click the connection and click Connect.

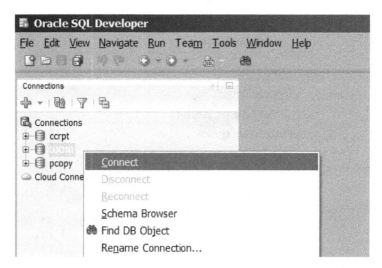

Note the name of the worksheet (tab label) is the name of your connection.

You can type source code on the worksheet.

Appendix A has the source code of all the book examples. Instead of typing, you can copy a source code and paste it on the worksheet.

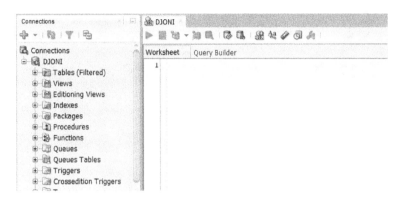

SQL Statement

Some of the book examples use a table named *produce*. Type in the SQL CREATE TABLE statement shown below to create the table (you might prefer to copy the *create_produce.sql* listing from Appendix A and paste it on your worksheet)

You run a SQL statement already in a worksheet by clicking the Run Statement button.

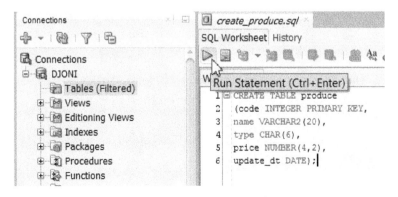

The Script Output pane confirms that the table has been created, and you should see the produce table in the Connection Navigator under your connection folder. If you don't see the newly created table, click Refresh.

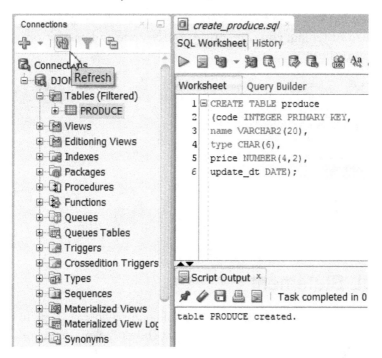

Inserting Rows

As an example of running multiple SQL statements in SQL Developer, the following five statements insert five rows into the produce table. Please type the statements, or copy it from *insert_produce.sql* in Appendix A. You will use these rows when you try the book examples.

Run all statements by clicking the Run Script button, or Ctrl+Enter (press and hold Ctrl button then click Enter button)

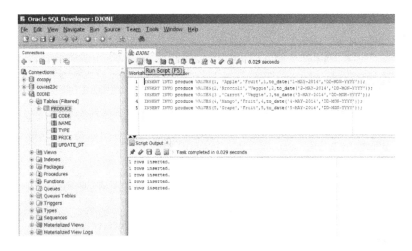

PL/SQL program

To learn how to run a PL/SQL program, type the following PL/SQL program, or copy it from *running_plsql.sql* in Appendix A.

You have not learned anything about PL/SQL programming yet, so don't worry what this program is all about.

To run the program, click the Run Script button or press F5.

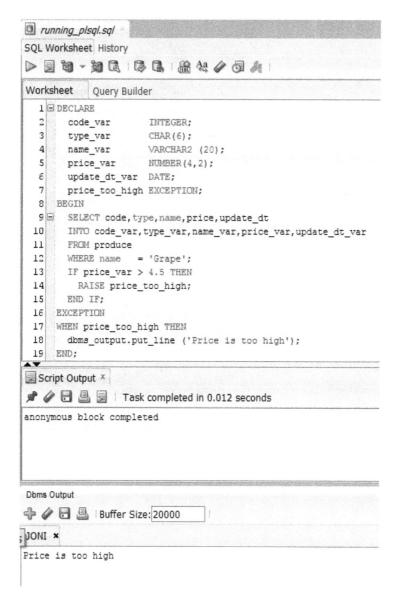

```
1  DECLARE
2     code_var        INTEGER;
3     type_var        CHAR(6);
4     name_var        VARCHAR2 (20);
5     price_var       NUMBER(4,2);
6     update_dt_var   DATE;
7     price_too_high  EXCEPTION;
8  BEGIN
9     SELECT code,type,name,price,update_dt
10    INTO code_var,type_var,name_var,price_var,update_dt_var
11    FROM produce
12    WHERE name    = 'Grape';
13    IF price_var > 4.5 THEN
14      RAISE price_too_high;
15    END IF;
16 EXCEPTION
17 WHEN price_too_high THEN
18    dbms_output.put_line ('Price is too high');
19 END;
```

Script Output ×

Task completed in 0.012 seconds

anonymous block completed

Dbms Output

Buffer Size: 20000

JONI ×

Price is too high

Multiple worksheets for a connection

Sometimes you need to have two or more programs on different worksheets. You can open more than one worksheet for a connection by right-clicking the connection and select Open SQL Worksheet.

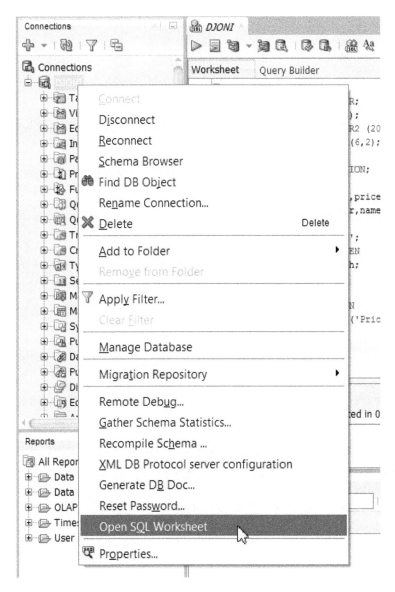

The names of the next tabs for a connection have sequential numbers added.

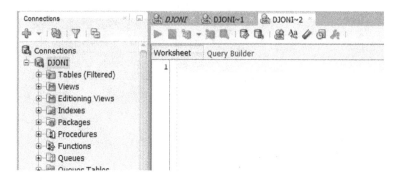

Storing the source code

You can store a source code into a text file for later re-opening
by selecting Save from the File menu.

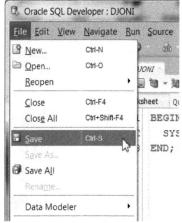

Select the location where you want to store the source code
and give the file a name, and then click Save.

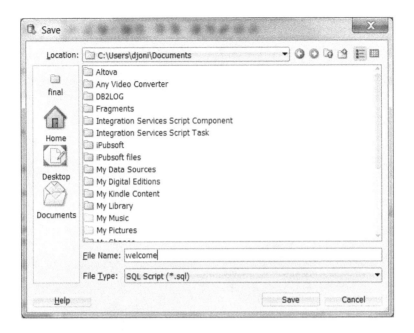

Opening a source code

You can open a source code by selecting Open or Reopen from the File menu and then select the file that contains the source code.

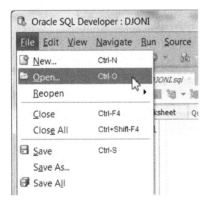

The source code will be opened on a new worksheet. The tab of the worksheet has the name of the file. The following is the worksheet opened for the source code stored as file named running_plsql.sql.

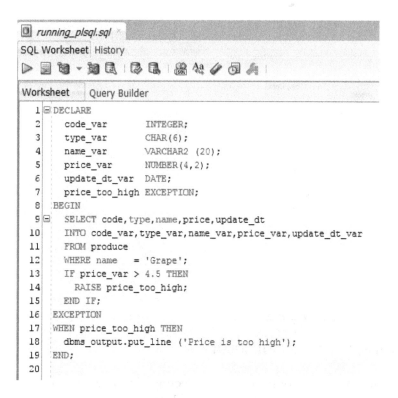

```
 1 ⊟ DECLARE
 2     code_var          INTEGER;
 3     type_var          CHAR(6);
 4     name_var          VARCHAR2 (20);
 5     price_var         NUMBER(4,2);
 6     update_dt_var     DATE;
 7     price_too_high EXCEPTION;
 8   BEGIN
 9 ⊟   SELECT code,type,name,price,update_dt
10       INTO code_var,type_var,name_var,price_var,update_dt_var
11       FROM produce
12       WHERE name   = 'Grape';
13       IF price_var > 4.5 THEN
14         RAISE price_too_high;
15       END IF;
16   EXCEPTION
17   WHEN price_too_high THEN
18     dbms_output.put_line ('Price is too high');
19   END;
20
```

Storing the listings in Appendix A into files

As an alternative to copy and paste, you can store each of the listing into a file and then you can open the file. Note that you must store each program source code into a file.

Running SQL or PL/SQL from a file

You can execute a file that contains SQL statement or PL/SQL program without opening it on the worksheet as shown here.

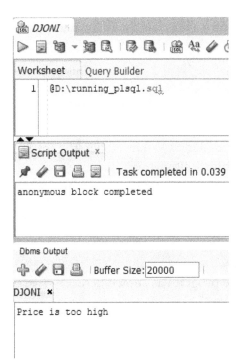

Clearing a Worksheet

To clear a Worksheet, click its Clear button.

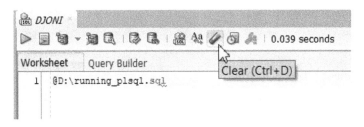

Displaying Output

Most of the book examples use the Oracle-supplied dbms_output.put_line procedure to display some outputs. For the book readers learning PL/SQL, the displayed output gives an instant feedback of what happens in the running program. Real-life programs might not need to display any output.

The dbms_output.put_line procedure has the following syntax.

dbms_output.put_line (parameter);

The value of the parameter must evaluate to a string literal (value).

When the procedure is executed in SQL Developer, the string literal is displayed on the Dbms Output.

To see the output, before you run the example, make sure you already have a Dbms Output pane opened for the connection you use to run the program. If your Dbms Output is not ready, set it up as follows:

Assume you want to run the program as shown here.

Click the View menu.

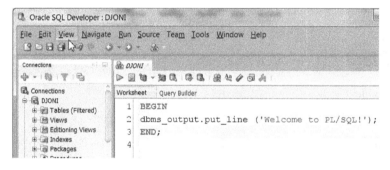

Next, select Dbms Output.

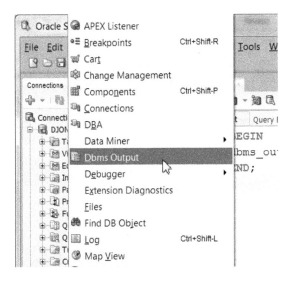

The Dbms Output pane is now opened.

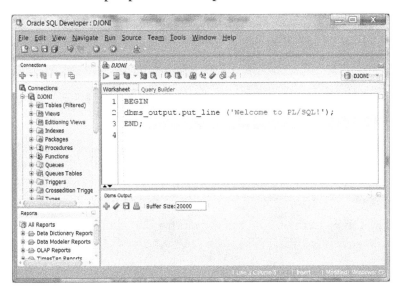

To display an output, you need to set up the Dbms Output pane for the connection you use to run the program. Click the + button on the Dbms Output pane.

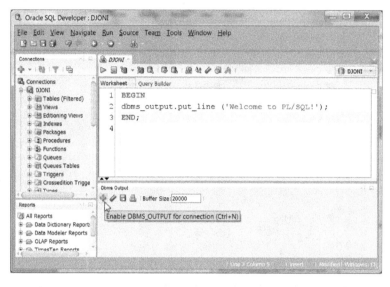

On the pop-up window, select the connection, and then click OK. As an example I select DJONI connection as this is the connection I want to use for running my PL/SQL program.

The Dbms Output now has the tab for the DJONI connection.

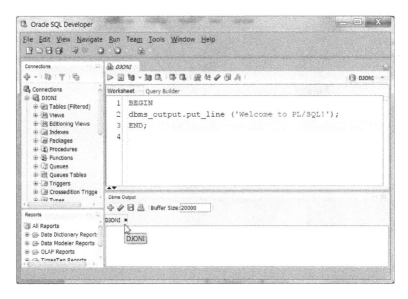

Now, run the program by clicking the Run Statement button. The Dbms Output pane displays the "Welcome to PL/SQL!" greeting. The message on the Script Output pane shows the result of running the program; in this case it indicates that the program is completed successfully. It would show an error message if the program is having a problem.

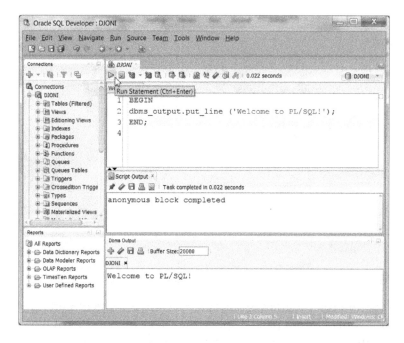

Clearing Dbms Output

To see a display output from a program, you might want to erase the output from a previous program. To clear a Dbms Output, click its Clear button.

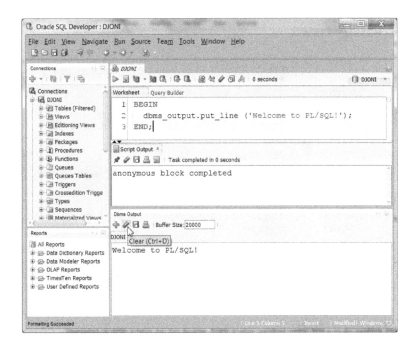

Appendix B: Inline Procedure and Function

Appendix C: Source Codes

The source codes listed here is in the alphabetical order of their names. The names are **bolded**. They are divided into four groups: product table, procedures, functions, and packages.

Product table

Creating product table

```
CREATE TABLE product
(p_code INTEGER PRIMARY KEY,
p_name VARCHAR2(20),
p_type CHAR(6),
price NUMBER(4,2),
update_dt DATE);
```

Adding rows

```
INSERT INTO product VALUES(1,
      'Apple','Fruit',1,to_date('1-MAY-2014','DD-MON-
      YYYY'));
INSERT INTO product
      VALUES(2,'Broccoli','Veggie',2,to_date('2-MAY-
      2014','DD-MON-YYYY'));
INSERT INTO product VALUES(3
      ,'Carrot','Veggie',3,to_date('3-MAY-2014','DD-
      MON-YYYY'));
INSERT INTO product
      VALUES(4,'Mango','Fruit',4,to_date('4-MAY-
      2014','DD-MON-YYYY'));
INSERT INTO product
      VALUES(5,'Grape','Fruit',5,to_date('5-MAY-
      2014','DD-MON-YYYY'));
INSERT INTO product VALUES(9,NULL,NULL,NULL,NULL);
```

Procedures

```
create or replace PROCEDURE BASIC_LOOP
AS
  num NUMBER := 1;
BEGIN
  LOOP
    IF num > 3 THEN -- loop three times only
      EXIT;
    END IF;
    DBMS_OUTPUT.PUT_LINE ('In loop: num = ' ||
      TO_CHAR(num));
    num := num + 1;
  END LOOP basic_loop;
  -- On EXIT, execute the following statement
  DBMS_OUTPUT.PUT_LINE('After loop: num = ' ||
      TO_CHAR(num));
END BASIC_LOOP;


create or replace PROCEDURE CODE_MSG
AS
  x VARCHAR2(5);
BEGIN
  x := 'abcdef';
EXCEPTION
```

```
WHEN VALUE_ERROR THEN
  dbms_output.put_line('The error code is: '
      ||SQLCODE);
  dbms_output.put_line('The error message is:
      '||SQLERRM);
END CODE_MSG;


create or replace PROCEDURE COM_RB
AS
  p_row product%ROWTYPE;
  price_count INTEGER := 0;
BEGIN
  SELECT * INTO p_row FROM product WHERE p_name =
      'Apple' FOR UPDATE OF price;
  UPDATE product SET price = 1.5 WHERE p_name =
      'Apple';
  SELECT COUNT(*) INTO price_count FROM product WHERE
      price = 1.5;
  IF price_count > 1 THEN
    ROLLBACK;
  ELSE
    COMMIT;
  END IF;
END COM_RB;

create or replace PROCEDURE COMBINED_EXCEPTION
AS
  code_v VARCHAR2(20);
BEGIN
  SELECT p_code INTO code_v FROM product WHERE p_name
      = 'Pineapple';
EXCEPTION
WHEN TOO_MANY_ROWS OR no_data_found THEN
  dbms_output.put_line ('Error with the Query');
END COMBINED_EXCEPTION;



create or replace PROCEDURE COMMENTS
AS
  /* An example stored procedure to show the two types
      of comment lines.
  This one is a multi-line comment
  */
BEGIN
```

```
    -- Use the built-in procedure to display a string (
        single-line comment)
    dbms_output.put_line( 'Hello, World'); -- a Hello,
        World (another single-line comment)
END COMMENTS;


create or replace PROCEDURE COMPUTATION
AS
  x DECIMAL(4,2) DEFAULT 1.1;
  y DECIMAL(4,2) ;
  z DECIMAL(4,2) DEFAULT 1.1;
BEGIN
  y := power ((x - 0.1) * 5 + (z + 0.9), 2) ;
  dbms_output.put_line (y);
END COMPUTATION;


create or replace PROCEDURE CURSOR_VIEW
AS
  product_rows product_view%rowtype;
BEGIN
  FOR cur IN
  ( SELECT * FROM product_view ORDER BY p_code
  )
  LOOP
    product_rows := cur;
    dbms_output.put_line (product_rows.p_code ||' '||
      product_rows.p_name||' '||product_rows.price);
  END LOOP;
END CURSOR_VIEW;


create or replace PROCEDURE DATA_TYPES
AS
  c  VARCHAR(5) DEFAULT 'MySQL';
  i  INTEGER(2) DEFAULT 99;
  n  NUMBER(4,2) DEFAULT 23.45;
  dt DATE DEFAULT '2014-09-20';
BEGIN
  dbms_output.put_line(c);
  dbms_output.put_line(i);
  dbms_output.put_line(n);
  dbms_output.put_line(dt);
END DATA_TYPES;
```

```
create or replace PROCEDURE DISPLAY_VARIABLE
AS
  greeting VARCHAR2(15) DEFAULT 'Hello, World!';
BEGIN
  dbms_output.put_line(greeting);
END DISPLAY_VARIABLE;


create or replace PROCEDURE EXC_INIT
AS
  pk_violation EXCEPTION;
  PRAGMA EXCEPTION_INIT(pk_violation, -1);
BEGIN
  UPDATE product SET p_code = 1 WHERE p_code = 2;
EXCEPTION
WHEN pk_violation THEN
  dbms_output.put_line (SQLCODE);
  dbms_output.put_line (SQLERRM);
END EXC_INIT;


create or replace PROCEDURE FIXED_ITERATION
AS
BEGIN
  FOR i IN 1..3
  LOOP
    dbms_output.put_line('Iteration number: '||i);
  END LOOP;
END FIXED_ITERATION;


create or replace PROCEDURE FOR_LOOP
AS
  CURSOR cur
  IS
    SELECT p_code, p_name FROM product WHERE p_type =
      'Veggie';
BEGIN
  FOR cur_index IN cur
  LOOP
    dbms_output.put_line(cur_index.p_code ||' '||
      cur_index.p_name);
  END LOOP;
END FOR_LOOP;
```

```
create or replace PROCEDURE FOR_UPDATE
AS
  p_row product%ROWTYPE;
  price_count INTEGER := 0;
BEGIN
  SELECT * INTO p_row FROM product WHERE p_name =
      'Apple' FOR UPDATE OF price;
  UPDATE product SET price = 1 WHERE p_name = 'Apple';
END FOR_UPDATE;


create or replace PROCEDURE HELLO_WORLD
AS
BEGIN
  dbms_output.put_line('Hello, World');
END HELLO_WORLD;


create or replace PROCEDURE IF_THEN(
    num_input NUMBER)
AS
BEGIN
  IF num_input > 10 THEN
    dbms_output.put_line(num_input || ' is greater
      than 10');
  END IF;
END IF_THEN;


create or replace PROCEDURE IF_THEN_BOOL(
    num_input NUMBER)
AS
  greater_than_10 BOOLEAN := num_input > 10;
BEGIN
  IF greater_than_10 THEN
    dbms_output.put_line(num_input || ' is greater
      than 10');
  END IF;
END IF_THEN_BOOL;


create or replace PROCEDURE IF_THEN_ELSE(
    num_input NUMBER)
AS
  greater_than_10 BOOLEAN := num_input > 10;
```

```
BEGIN
  IF greater_than_10 THEN
    dbms_output.put_line(num_input || ' is greater
      than 10');
  ELSE
    dbms_output.put_line(num_input || ' is less than
      10');
  END IF;
END IF_THEN_ELSE;


create or replace PROCEDURE IF_THEN_ELSIF(
    num_input NUMBER)
AS
  greater_than_10 BOOLEAN := num_input > 10;
BEGIN
  IF greater_than_10 THEN
    dbms_output.put_line(num_input || ' is greater
      than 10');
  ELSIF num_input = 10 THEN
    dbms_output.put_line(num_input || ' is equal to
      10');
  ELSE
    dbms_output.put_line(num_input || ' is less than
      10');
  END IF;
END IF_THEN_ELSIF;


create or replace PROCEDURE INCREASE_10PCT
AS
  avg_price NUMBER;
BEGIN
  SELECT AVG(price) INTO avg_price FROM product;
  dbms_output.put_line('The average price is: ' ||
      avg_price);
  UPDATE product SET price = price + 0.1 * avg_price
      WHERE price < avg_price;
END INCREASE_10PCT;


create or replace PROCEDURE INCREASE_PRICE(
    CODE     IN VARCHAR2 ,
    INCREASE IN NUMBER )
AS
BEGIN
```

```
    UPDATE product SET price = price + (price *
        increase/100) WHERE p_code = code;
END INCREASE_PRICE;


create or replace PROCEDURE INTO_CLAUSE
AS
  code_v  VARCHAR2(20);
  name_v  VARCHAR2(20);
  price_v NUMBER(6,2);
BEGIN
  SELECT p_code, p_name,
    price
  INTO code_v, name_v,
    price_v
  FROM product
  WHERE p_name = 'Apple';
  dbms_output.put_line( 'The price of our ' ||name_v||
      ' (its code is '||(code_v)|| ') is $' ||
      price_v);
END INTO_CLAUSE;


create or replace PROCEDURE INVALID_VARIABLE_NAME
AS
  bad@name VARCHAR2(10);
BEGIN
  NULL;
END INVALID_VARIABLE_NAME;


create or replace PROCEDURE IS_OPEN
AS
  CURSOR cur
  IS
    SELECT p_name FROM product;
  name_c VARCHAR2(5);
  s      VARCHAR2(15);
BEGIN
  OPEN cur;
  LOOP
    FETCH cur INTO name_c;
    EXIT
  WHEN cur%notfound;
  END LOOP;
EXCEPTION
```

```
WHEN OTHERS THEN
  IF cur%ISOPEN THEN
    s := 'c is still Open';
    dbms_output.put_line(s);
    dbms_output.put_line(SQLERRM);
  END IF;
  CLOSE cur;
END IS_OPEN;


create or replace PROCEDURE LAST_ROW
AS
  CURSOR cur
  IS
    SELECT * FROM product;
  product_rows cur%rowtype;
  i INTEGER := 1;
BEGIN
  OPEN cur;
  WHILE i < 7
  LOOP
    FETCH cur INTO product_rows;
    dbms_output.put_line(product_rows.p_code);
    i := i + 1;
  END LOOP;
  CLOSE cur;
END LAST_ROW;


create or replace PROCEDURE LOCAL_TS
AS
  ts TIMESTAMP DEFAULT localtimestamp;
BEGIN
  dbms_output.put_line(ts);
END LOCAL_TS;


create or replace PROCEDURE MAIN
AS
BEGIN
  hello_world;
  data_types;
  display_variable;
END MAIN;
```

```
create or replace PROCEDURE MULTI_HANDLER
AS
  code_v VARCHAR2(20);
BEGIN
  SELECT p_code INTO code_v FROM product WHERE p_name
      = 'Pineapple';
EXCEPTION
WHEN TOO_MANY_ROWS THEN
  dbms_output.put_line ('Too many rows exception');
WHEN OTHERS THEN
  dbms_output.put_line ('Other exception');
END MULTI_HANDLER;


create or replace PROCEDURE MULTIPLE_ROWS
AS
  code_v  VARCHAR2(20);
  name_v  VARCHAR2(20);
  price_v NUMBER(6,2);
BEGIN
  SELECT p_code, p_name, price INTO code_v, name_v,
      price_v FROM product;
  dbms_output.put_line( 'The price of our ' ||name_v||
      ' (its code is '||(code_v)|| ') is $' ||
      price_v);
--EXCEPTION
--WHEN too_many_rows THEN
--  dbms_output.put_line('Error: More than one row
      returned');
END MULTIPLE_ROWS;


create or replace PROCEDURE NESTED_LOOP
AS
  counter1 NUMBER := 1;
  counter2 NUMBER := 1;
BEGIN
  LOOP
    IF counter1 > 2 THEN
      EXIT; -- loop twice
    END IF;
    DBMS_OUTPUT.PUT_LINE ('Outer loop: counter1 = ' ||
      TO_CHAR(counter1));
    counter1 := counter1 + 1;
    LOOP
      IF counter2 > 2 THEN
```

```
      EXIT; -- loop twice
    END IF;
    DBMS_OUTPUT.PUT_LINE ('Inner loop: counter2 = '
    || TO_CHAR(counter2));
    counter2 := counter2 + 1;
  END LOOP;
  counter2 := 1;
  END LOOP;
  DBMS_OUTPUT.PUT_LINE('After loop: counter1 = ' ||
    TO_CHAR(counter1));
END NESTED_LOOP;


create or replace PROCEDURE NO_DECLARATION
AS
BEGIN
  dbms_output.put_line(greeting);
END NO_DECLARATION;


create or replace PROCEDURE NO_ROW
AS
  product_row product%rowtype;
BEGIN
  SELECT * INTO product_row FROM product WHERE p_name
    = 'Pineapple';
  dbms_output.put_line (product_row.p_code);
END NO_ROW;


create or replace PROCEDURE NO_ROW_EXCEPTION
AS
  product_row product%rowtype;
BEGIN
  SELECT * INTO product_row FROM product WHERE p_name
    = 'Pineapple';
  dbms_output.put_line (product_row.p_code);
EXCEPTION
WHEN no_data_found THEN
  dbms_output.put_line('Our product does not have any
    Pineapple');
END NO_ROW_EXCEPTION;


create or replace PROCEDURE NOT_FOUND
AS
```

```
  CURSOR cur
  IS
    SELECT * FROM product;
  product_rows cur%rowtype;
BEGIN
  OPEN cur;
  LOOP
    FETCH cur INTO product_rows;
    EXIT
  WHEN cur%notfound;
    dbms_output.put_line(product_rows.p_code || ' - '
      || product_rows.p_name);
  END LOOP;
  CLOSE cur;
END NOT_FOUND;


create or replace PROCEDURE PRODUCT_CUR
AS
  CURSOR cur
  IS
    SELECT * FROM product;
  product_rows cur%rowtype; -- declared having the
      cursor's type
BEGIN
  OPEN cur;
  FETCH cur INTO product_rows;
  dbms_output.put_line(product_rows.p_code || ' ' ||
      product_rows.p_name);
END PRODUCT_CUR;


create or replace PROCEDURE SEARCHED_CASE
AS
  max_price NUMBER;
  avg_price NUMBER;
BEGIN
  SELECT MAX(price) INTO max_price FROM product;
  SELECT AVG(price) INTO avg_price FROM product;
  dbms_output.put_line( max_price || avg_price);
  CASE
  WHEN max_price > 5 THEN
    UPDATE product SET price = price - (price * 0.1);
  WHEN avg_price < 3.5 THEN
    UPDATE product SET price = price + (price * 0.1);
  END CASE;
```

```
END SEARCHED_CASE;


create or replace PROCEDURE SET_VAR
AS
  w VARCHAR(25) DEFAULT 'PL/SQL';
BEGIN
  w := CONCAT('Welcome to ', w);
  dbms_output.put_line (w);
END SET_VAR;


create or replace PROCEDURE SHORT_CUT
AS
  output VARCHAR2(40);
BEGIN
  FOR product_rows IN
  (SELECT * FROM product
  )
  LOOP
    output := 'The name of this ' ||
       product_rows.p_type || ' is: ' ||
       product_rows.p_name;
    dbms_output.put_line(output);
  END LOOP;
END SHORT_CUT;


create or replace PROCEDURE SIMPLE_CASE(
    clue IN VARCHAR2 )
AS
BEGIN
  CASE clue
  WHEN 'O' THEN
    dbms_output.put_line('Obvious');
  WHEN 'U' THEN
    dbms_output.put_line('Useless');
  WHEN 'NS' THEN
    dbms_output.put_line('Not Sure');
  WHEN 'NM' THEN
    dbms_output.put_line('Need More');
  ELSE
    dbms_output.put_line('Input Not Valid');
  END CASE;
END SIMPLE_CASE;
```

```
create or replace PROCEDURE SPECIAL_DATATYPES
AS
   avg_price product.price%TYPE;
   p_row product%ROWTYPE;
BEGIN
   SELECT * INTO p_row FROM product WHERE p_name =
       'Carrot';
   dbms_output.put_line('The price of our
       '||p_row.p_name ||' (its code is
       '||p_row.p_code|| ') is $'||p_row.price);
END SPECIAL_DATATYPES;


create or replace PROCEDURE SQL_STATEMENTS
AS
BEGIN
   INSERT INTO product VALUES
     (9999, 'Test', NULL, NULL, NULL
     );
   UPDATE product SET price = 0 WHERE p_code = 9999;
   DELETE FROM product WHERE p_code = 9;
END SQL_STATEMENTS;


create or replace PROCEDURE USER_EXC
AS
   product_row product%ROWTYPE;
   price_too_high EXCEPTION;
BEGIN
   SELECT * INTO product_row FROM product WHERE p_name
       = 'Grape';
   IF product_row.price > 4.5 THEN
     RAISE price_too_high;
   END IF;
EXCEPTION
WHEN price_too_high THEN
   dbms_output.put_line('Price too high');
END USER_EXC;


create or replace PROCEDURE VAL_ERR
AS
   x VARCHAR2(5);
BEGIN
   x := 'abcdef';
```

```
    dbms_output.put_line('Error');
EXCEPTION
WHEN VALUE_ERROR THEN
    dbms_output.put_line ('We have an error related to
        data value');
END VAL_ERR;


create or replace PROCEDURE VALUE_ERROR
AS
    x VARCHAR2(5);
BEGIN
    x := 'abcdef';
    dbms_output.put_line('Error');
EXCEPTION
WHEN VALUE_ERROR THEN
    dbms_output.put_line ('We have an error related to
        data value');
END VALUE_ERROR;


create or replace PROCEDURE VARIABLE_IN_CUR
AS
    price_increase NUMBER(2,2) := 0.01;
    CURSOR cur
    IS
        SELECT price, (price + price_increase) new_price
            FROM product;
    price_rows cur%rowtype;
BEGIN
    OPEN cur;
    FETCH cur INTO price_rows;
    dbms_output.put_line('The current price of ' ||
        price_rows.price || ' will increase to ' ||
        price_rows.new_price);
END VARIABLE_IN_CUR;


create or replace PROCEDURE WHILE_LOOP
AS
    i INTEGER := 1;
BEGIN
    WHILE i < 4
    LOOP
        dbms_output.put_line('Iteration number: '||i);
        i := i +1;
```

```
    END LOOP;
END WHILE_LOOP;
```

Functions

```
create or replace FUNCTION NEW_PRICE(
    CURRENT_PRICE IN NUMBER ,
    INCREASE      IN NUMBER )
  RETURN NUMBER
AS
  new_price NUMBER(8,2);
BEGIN
  new_price := current_price + (current_price *
     increase);
  RETURN new_price;
END NEW_PRICE;


create or replace FUNCTION MULTI_RETURN(
    CURRENT_PRICE IN NUMBER ,
    INCREASE      IN NUMBER )
  RETURN NUMBER
AS
  new_price NUMBER(8,2);
  -- return_val new_price%type;
BEGIN
  new_price    := current_price + (current_price *
     increase);
  IF new_price <= 3.5 THEN
    RETURN new_price;
  ELSE
    RETURN current_price;
  END IF;
END multi_return;


create or replace FUNCTION WITH_SQL(
    CURRENT_PRICE IN NUMBER ,
    INCREASE      IN NUMBER )
  RETURN NUMBER
AS
  new_price NUMBER(8,2);
  avg_price product.price%type;
BEGIN
  SELECT AVG(price) INTO avg_price FROM product;
```

```
    new_price := current_price + (avg_price * increase);
    RETURN new_price;
END WITH_SQL;


create or replace FUNCTION WITH_EXCEPTION(
    CURRENT_PRICE IN NUMBER ,
    INCREASE      IN NUMBER )
  RETURN NUMBER
AS
  price_too_high EXCEPTION;
  new_price       NUMBER(8,2);
  avg_price product.price%type;
BEGIN
  SELECT AVG(price) INTO avg_price FROM product;
  new_price    := current_price + (avg_price *
      increase);
  IF new_price > 5 THEN
    RAISE price_too_high;
  ELSE
    RETURN new_price;
  END IF;
EXCEPTION
WHEN price_too_high THEN
  RETURN 1;
END WITH_EXCEPTION;
```

Package

```
CREATE OR REPLACE PACKAGE PRICING
AS
  PROCEDURE INCREASE_PRICE(
      CODE     IN VARCHAR2 ,
      INCREASE IN NUMBER );
  PROCEDURE INCREASE_10PCT;
  FUNCTION NEW_PRICE(
      CURRENT_PRICE IN NUMBER ,
      INCREASE      IN NUMBER )
    RETURN NUMBER;
END PRICING;
```